Nature Walks
with Culture Talks

走讀自然
花言樹語
台北植物生態與人文

蘇正隆 著

國家圖書館出版品預行編目資料

走讀自然．花言樹語 = Nature Walks with Culture Talks / 蘇正隆著. -- 一版. – 台北市：書林出版有限公司, 2025.1
面； 公分

ISBN 978-626-7605-04-2（平裝）

1.CST: 人文地理 2.CST: 植物 3.CST: 台北市

33.9/101.4　　　　　　　　　　　　　　113018401

走讀自然．花言樹語
Nature Walks with Culture Talks

作　　　者	蘇正隆
繪　　　者	鄭杏倩
編　　　輯	張雅雯
出　版　者	書林出版有限公司
	100台北市羅斯福路四段60號3樓
	Tel (02) 2368-4938．2365-8517　　Fax (02) 2368-8929．2363-6630
台北書林書店	106台北市新生南路三段88號2樓之5　　Tel (02) 2365-8517
學校業務部	Tel (02) 2368-7226．(04) 2376-3799．(07) 229-0300
經銷業務部	Tel (02) 2368-4938
發　行　人	蘇正隆
郵　　　撥	15743873．書林出版有限公司
網　　　址	http://www.bookman.com.tw
登　記　證	局版臺業字第一八三一號
出 版 日 期	2025年1月一版初刷
定　　　價	350元（US$15.00）
I　S　B　N	978-626-7605-04-2

本書由臺北市政府文化局贊助出版。

台北市文化局
TAIPEI Department of Cultural Affairs
Taipei City Government

欲利用本書全部或部分內容者，須徵得書林出版有限公司同意或書面授權。
請洽書林出版部，Tel (02) 2368-4938。

出版說明

　　本書介紹 10 條台北市區及近郊適合植物、生態、人文觀察的〈走讀自然〉路線，以及收錄 48 篇〈花言樹語〉，從跨領域的視角，談植物、生態、中西文學、名稱由來、學名字源解說與相關翻譯。

　　〈走讀自然〉部分都附有英文簡介及沿途動植物的中英文名稱，方便英語導覽及跨學科 CILL 參考教材。書中動植物英文名稱大多根據最新研究，仔細考證。對從事翻譯者在碰到植物名稱有許多譯法，莫衷一是時，也有所助益。

　　以「茄苳」為例，目前最大的網路植物資料庫「認識植物」(http://kplant.biodiv.tw/) 列了以下三種英文名稱：Autummn Maple Tree、Red Cedar、Toog tree，但都不可靠，除 Autummn Maple [sic] 拼錯外，透過 Google 搜索：

　　Autumn Maple 出現的都是秋天的楓樹 (*Acer* spp.)；Red Cedar 則是指柏科的 *Juniperus virginiana* 或 *Thuja plicata*。(Red cedar is a member of the cypress family, *Cupressaceae*, which also includes redwoods and sequoias.)；Toog tree 是指玉蕊科的 *Petersianthus quadrialatus*。

　　我們提供的是英美植物學界採用、最貼近學名 *Bischofia javanica* 的 Javanese Bishopwood，簡稱 Bishopwood。

再以台灣常見的繡眼鳥科鳥類「綠繡眼」為例，目前牠已從 *Zosterops japonicas* 分出，學名為 *Zosterops simplex*，正式名稱為「斯氏繡眼」(Swinhoe's White-eye)，而以前的英文名稱 Warbling White-eye 則專指「日菲繡眼」(*Zosterops japonicas*)。

〈走讀自然〉中所列出的植物有數百種，〈花言樹語〉中只介紹了 60 餘種，其餘植物大多可以從書林出版、陳文彬著的《新細說台灣原生植物》和《看見台灣原生植物》兩本圖鑑中找到詳細的圖文介紹。

前言　　植物因緣

　　讀中學時我就對國文、英文課本內出現的植物很好奇，希望能多認識。我大學讀外文系，喜歡登山，周末幾乎都在山野觀察植物。但在 1975 年前，想要認識台灣周遭的本地植物，坊間幾乎沒有甚麼植物圖鑑可查。平常在野外觀察到的植物，只能憑記憶到台大總圖書館翻查不能外借的《植物大辭典》(1918 年出版) 或清代的《植物名實圖考》之類圖書來印證。後來我發現台大研究圖書館藏有日治時代的《台灣野生食用植物圖譜》，雖然插圖只是簡單的黑白線條畫，但比起《植物大辭典》之類對我要有用的多。這樣自修摸索了三年，也認識了一些植物。不過這樣的自習畢竟不夠，因此我大四時到植物系所去修分類學家 (plant taxonomist) 許建昌教授開的「雜草學」(Weeds)。除了跟許教授到野外認識植物外，大四那年我大部分時間多待在許老師的禾本科 (*Poaceae*) 研究室。同一研究室還有研究生彭鏡毅，他去野外採集時，有時由我帶路，也從他那裡學到不少。

　　那時台灣規劃興建中山高速公路，委託許教授做公路兩旁護坡草本植栽研究。許老師派給我的任務是去採集幾十種草本植物的種子，並觀察統計它們在日照及無日照情況下的萌芽率 (Germination in light and in darkness)。所以我每天都待到晚上 12 點，觀察統計好研究室暗房裡植物種子的萌芽情況才走。

由於比一般人稍微多認識一些植物，大學期間政大、台大登山隊在嚮導訓練營時都曾找我去介紹野外求生植物，大學畢業，1977 年服完兵役，書林尚未創立前，我從事翻譯、寫作，為《戶外生活》雜誌撰寫《大屯山植物觀察旅行》、《銀河洞植物觀察旅行》等專欄，算是自然生態觀察旅行的先驅。

　　1996 年，台北市龍安國小在臺大昆蟲系石正人教授規劃下，成立生物營。1997 年，由我擔任植物營營長，在台大植物系郭城孟教授的指導下，我帶領熱心的家長吳寶珠、陳麗貞等利用暑假做溫州社區植物普查，將其中的植物資源標示出來，由黃蓉美主編、陳永明繪圖，製成全臺第一份社區自然步道地圖。此外，我們也發行《溫州花言樹語》刊物，「花言樹語」一詞是主編黃蓉美所創的，我後來寫植物專欄就一直沿用，不敢掠美，在此一併交代。

　　我不是科班出身的植物學家，但我導覽時比較常注入中西文學、環境與社會、外語、翻譯等元素，因此也頗受歡迎，國內外都有不少學校邀我去導覽。還有一位美國學者 Dr. Wiley Blevins，因為聽了我的導覽，立志寫一本給青少年的植物科普書，後來 Ninja Plants 一書出版了，書的扉頁赫然寫著「獻給 Jerome Su」(To Jerome Su, who inspired this book after our walk through the campus grounds of National Taiwan University in Taipei)。

　　這幾年來我在臉書上撰寫〈花言樹語〉，經常收到李振清教授、陳東榮教授、王安琪教授的鼓勵及詢問何時結集出版？感謝臺北市文化局的贊助，藉此機會，將近年來幾十場〈走讀自然〉中的 10 條路線，以及臉書上 48 篇〈花言樹語〉，重新修訂改寫。儘量參考最新的研究，增加學名的註解，希望對喜好植物、關心生態、英文導覽、CLIL 英語教學以及翻譯工作者有所幫助。

最後要感謝書林企劃王才宜策畫近年來的走讀自然活動及申請專案；植物分類專家台大植物標本館鄭淑芬技正多年來協助鑑識植物；香港城市大學語言與翻譯系林楚皓同學及書林同事沈愛萍協助，蒐集我寫過的相關文章；編輯張雅雯爬梳整理；台灣師大翻譯研究所嚴浩文、彭國欣、劉驊、賴彥瑜、Lorraine McShea、Kyle Rice、王裕忠、彭心玗、林婉菁、林品妤、陳瑟娟、吳佳謙等同學提供自然步道英文簡介，以及台大外文系賀安莉 (Ann-Marie Hadzima) 教授協助修訂英文，讓本書能以現在的面貌呈現，衷心感謝。

本書〈植物的葉子〉、〈花事知多少？〉兩篇介紹花與葉的專文轉載自陳文彬《看見台灣原生植物》、《新細說台灣原生植物》（書林），亦一併致謝。

目次 Table of Contents

- i　　出版說明
- iii　　前言　植物因緣

【走讀自然】

- 002　**1 寶藏巖**
  造訪城市綠色藝術人文部落
  Treasure Trove Tree Talk & Culture Walk

- 008　**2 台大校園**
  校園植物與人文自然巡禮
  Plants in Literature: Walk Through the Campus Grounds of National Taiwan University

- 018　**3 溫州社區 / 殷海光故居**
  社區自然資源與人文記憶
  Meander Down the Historic and Cultural Walk of Taipei's Wenzhou Community

- 026　**4 瑠公圳 / 霧裡薛圳**
  探尋水圳，看見原生水濱植物
  Liugongzun & Wulixue Canal: The City's Historic Irrigation System and the Variety of Aquatic Life

- 034　**5 芝山岩 / 北隘門步道**
  滄海桑田，千萬年岩丘中的秘密
  Zhishan Yan—Stories Spanning Millions of Years Found in Sandstone

040	**6 仙跡岩**	
	鬧市仙居的生態人文探索	
	Xianji Rock Trail: Flora, Fauna, and Literature	
046	**7 象山**	
	走過侏儸紀活化石林，俯瞰台北	
	Xiangshan Hiking Trail: Flora, Fauna, and Fiction	
052	**8 虎山**	
	走過山澗步道，多識草木鳥獸之名	
	Hushan Hiking Trail: Plants in Literature	
060	**9 軍艦岩**	
	發現植物人文與地質的美	
	Discover Beitou's Battleship Rock: A Hike Amongst Nature's Marvels	
065	**10 林語堂故居 / 尾崙古圳 / 狗殷勤古道**	
	循先人足跡探訪文學中的植物	
	The Lin Yutang House, Gouyinqin Ancient Trail & Plants in Literature	
073	**植物的葉子**	陳文彬
083	**花事知多少？**	陳文彬

【花言樹語】

094	談植物的學名及字源
100	附生與寄生
103	鳥榕，雀榕與纏勒
106	薜荔與愛玉
109	都是麵包樹惹的禍
114	西番蓮、百香果與毛西番蓮

117	流蘇
119	從苦苓、苦楝到戀樹
122	從台灣連翹到金露花
124	話說鳳梨
128	海芋與美人蕉
130	新興水果：黃金果與牛奶果
133	檸檬與萊姆
135	橘子與橙
137	阿勃勒、台灣欒樹、金鍊花
140	台灣欒樹
144	辛夷/紫玉蘭與木芙蓉
146	馬拉巴栗
149	蓮霧，釋迦，粉介殼蟲
153	白千層
155	松柏類樹木的英文
156	別再炒作落羽杉
159	野薑花是古巴國花
162	青花菜與花椰菜
166	印度棗，中國棗，海棗/椰棗
168	石榴，石榴石與音位/字位轉換
170	新興蔬果：木鱉果
173	櫟樹、橡實、伊比利豬
176	火球花
178	母親的花：康乃馨與金針花

180	夜來花香──晚香玉及夜香木
183	黃花風鈴木與黃鐘花
185	愛文芒果與麗蠅
188	緬梔與梔子
192	曇花一現
194	綬草
195	茄苳、重陽木、金城武樹
197	復活節的植物：漆姑草、鳳仙、酢醬草
201	福木
203	**楓香**
206	木棉與吉貝木棉
209	肉豆蔻、小豆蔻、豆蔻年華
213	杏仁豆腐、杏仁茶英文怎麼說？
215	芋頭與南島民族
217	柿子挑軟的吃
219	甜品葷與素：吉利丁、果膠與瓊膠
222	野菜
225	檳榔、半天花、半天筍、荖藤的英文
227	後語

走讀自然

路線1 寶藏巖

造訪城市綠色藝術人文部落
Treasure Trove Tree Talk & Culture Walk

Located by the Xindian River, Treasure Trove (Temple) community used to have extensive urban farms between the settlement and the river.

From its origins as a squatter settlement in the 1940s, Treasure Trove (Temple) community since 2010 has transformed into an eco-friendly art village and featured in *The New York Times* as one of Taiwan's must-see destinations.

Known for its narrow alleyways and colorful murals, the community presents a unique blend of not only contemporary art, but also other cultural exhibitions as well as other examples of historic preservation. Visitors can explore the numerous art installations, galleries, and performance venues throughout the village.

Transportation

By MRT: Take the green line to MRT Gongguan Station. From there, take Exit 1 and walk to the Treasure Hill（寶藏巖）.

寶藏巖位於新店溪畔、福和橋旁,倚靠昔稱拳山,今稱為小觀音山而建,最高點 80 公尺,為臺北最古老的寺廟之一,因依山崖而建,故稱為「巖」,但不是岩石的岩。

寶藏巖台北市官方的英譯是 Treasure Hill，意思是寶山、寶丘，我覺得譯為 Treasure Trove 更有尋寶、探秘的意味，而且押頭韻，會更吸引人。根據牛津辭典 Treasure Trove 的意思是：a collection or store of valuable or delightful things. "the website provides a treasure trove of information about the county's heritage"，因此我的寶藏巖植物與人文導覽，英文標題為 Treasure Trove Tree Talk & Culture Walk。

由台北捷運公館站 1 號出口，走汀州路 3 段 200 巷到巷底水源町公園，上小觀音山木棧道，約 400 公尺，即可抵達創建於 1791 年（乾隆 56 年）的寶藏巖觀音寺，過了寺廟，就是寶藏巖聚落國際藝術村。

寶藏巖聚落係戰後由榮民、城鄉移民與都市原住民等社會弱勢族群，於公館邊緣地區新店溪旁小觀音山南側違建造屋所形成的聚落，頗有歷史特色。雖然面積只有 3.97 公頃，但擁有特殊人文景觀，小觀音山木板道沿途綠意盎然，動植物種類繁多，生態資源豐富。

1980-1990 年代，台北市政府以整頓市容等理由，計劃拆除聚落，不過遭到居民陳情抗議。1997 年台大城鄉所師生積極介入，才受到普遍注意。2006 年《紐約時報》將該寶藏巖聚落納入台北最具特色的景點之一。2011 年臺北市文化局公告「寶藏巖聚落」為歷史聚落。

目前聚落建物約 87 戶，規劃為「寶藏家園」、「藝術家駐村」及「國際青年會所」三大主題區，以「聚落活保存」為目標。「寶村柑仔店」由原住戶約 20 戶的居民後代組成之寶藏家園與藝術村所經營，強化「藝居共生」，透過第二代居民逐漸回流經營聚落。

🌿 木棧道沿途植物

稜果榕 (*Ficus septica*) White-veined Fig/Septic Fig、構樹 Paper Mulberry、血桐 Blush Macaranga/David's Heart、姑婆芋 (*Alocasia odora*) Giant Elephant's Ear、月桃 (*Alpinia zerumbet*) Shell Ginger、島榕 (*Ficus virgata*) Twiggy Fig、葛藤 Kudzu、桑樹 Mulberry、山棕 (*Arenga engleri*) Taiwan Sugar Palm、山黃麻 (*Trema tomentosa*) Oriental trema、野牡丹 (*Melastoma candidum*) Common Melastoma、香楠 (*Machilus zuihoensis*) Incense Machilus、合果芋 Arrowhead Plant/Arrowhead Vine、黃金葛 (*Epipremnum aureum*) Golden Pothos、風藤 (*Piper kadsura*) Kadsura Pepper、麵包樹 (*Artocarpus treculinus*) Breadfruit、鵝掌柴/鴨腳木 (江某) (*Schefflera octophylla*) Common Schefflera、朱蕉 (*Cordyline fruticosa*) Ti Plant、山葡萄 (*Ampelopsis glandulosa*) Amur Peppervine/Wild Grape

稜果榕 (*Ficus septica*) 葉片兩面光滑，葉脈偏黃、明顯。

水同木 (*Ficus fistulosa*) Common Yellow Stem-fig 葉面光滑，葉背有柔毛，葉脈與葉肉顏色差別不大。

▲ 圖 1 山葡萄 (*Ampelopsis glandulosa*)

▲ 圖 2 稜果榕 (*Ficus septica*)

寶藏巖入口右前方山坡次生林的植物

蒴藋/有骨消 (*Sambucus chinensis*) Taiwan Elderberry、白花蛇舌草 Snake-needle Grass、牽牛花 Morning Glory、木苧麻 False-nettle

入口處花台的植栽

日日櫻 (*Jatropha pandurifolia*) Rose-flowered Nettlespurge、地瓜 (*Ipomoea batatas*) Sweet Potato、樹蘭 (*Aglaia odorata*) Chinese Perfume Tree、月橘/七里香 (*Murraya paniculata*) Common Jasmine Orange、蕺菜/魚腥草 (*Houttuynia cordata*) Fish Mint、五蕊油柑 (*Phyllanthus tenellus*) Mascarene Island Leaf-flower

寶藏巖崗哨周遭

楊桃 (*Averrhoa carambola*) Carambola/Star Fruit、龍眼 (*Dimocarpus longan*) Longan、山菜豆 (*Radermachera sinica*) China Doll/Serpent Tree

寶村柑仔店、三角窗服務台周遭植物

雀榕 (*Ficus subpisocarpa*) Deciduous Fig、山菜豆 (*Radermachera sinica*) China Doll/Serpent Tree、飛揚草 (*Euphorbia hirta*) Hairy Spurge/Asthma Weed、黃椰子 (*Chrysalidocarpus lutescens*) Yellow Palm/Areca Palm、朴樹 (*Celtis sinensis*) Chinese Hackberry、綠竹 (*Bambusa oldhamii*) Green Bamboo

停車場、菜園周遭植物

芒果樹 (*Mangifera indica*) Mango、光蠟樹/白雞油 (*Fraxinus formosana*) Griffith's Ash/Formosan Ash、串鼻龍 Gourian Clematis、百香果 (*Passiflora edulis*) Passion Fruit、榕樹 (*Ficus microcarpa*) Chinese Banyan、In Hong Kong, it is called 細葉榕、樟樹 Camphor Tree、白千層 (*Melaleuca leucadendra*) Weeping Paperbark、第倫桃 (*Dillenia indica*) Elephant Apple、番石榴/芭樂 (*Psidium guajava*) Guava

蔓花生 (*Arachis duranensis*) Wild Peanut、蘆筍 (*Asparagus officinalis*) Asparagus、落葵/皇宮菜 (*Basella alba*) Vine Spinach、木瓜 (*Carica papaya*) Papaya、萵苣 (*Lactuca sativa*) Lettuce、辣椒 (*Capsicum*) Chili Pepper、印度橡膠 (*Capsicum*) Indian Rubber Tree

山藥 Yam、紅藜 (*Chenopodium formosanum*) Taiwan Red Quinoa/Djulis、金針 (*Hemerocallis citrina*) Orange Daylily、破布子 (*Cordia dichotoma*) Cordia/Fragrant Manjack、洛神花 (*Hibiscus sabdariffa*) Roselle、台灣欒樹 (*Koelreuteria formosana*) Taiwan Goldenrain Tree、烏桕 (*Triadica sebifera*) Chinese Tallow、菠蘿蜜 (*Artocarpus heterophyllus*) Jackfruit

小葉欖仁 (*Terminalia mantalyi*) Madagascar Almond、榔榆/紅雞油 (*Ulmus parvifolia*) Chinese Elm、青剛櫟 (*Quercus glauca*) Ring-cupped Oak

▲ 寶藏巖一景 沿斜坡往下走後即往停車場（張雅雯 攝）

導覽地圖

- 汀州路三段
- 200巷
- 230巷
- 小觀音山木棧道
- 寶藏巖入口
- 入口處花台
- 有骨消、構樹、血桐
- 白花蛇舌草、姑婆芋
- 牽牛花、葛藤、木苧麻
- 日日櫻、地瓜葉
- 樹蘭、七里香
- 寶藏巖寺
- 七里香、山菜豆
- 魚腥草、五蕊油柑
- 楊桃
- 龍眼
- 警衛室
- 芒果樹、光臘樹
- 串鼻龍、百香果
- 榕樹
- 籃球場
- 蔓花生、桑樹、蘆筍
- 落葵、木瓜、高苣、辣椒
- 姑婆芋、印度橡膠
- 三角國服務站
- 寶藏巖柑仔店
- 辣椒、山藥、紅藜
- 金針、破布子、洛神花
- 台灣欒樹
- 停車場
- 榔榆
- 飛揚草
- 山菜豆、雀榕、構樹
- 小葉欖仁
- 黃椰子
- 芒果
- 綠竹、朴樹
- 青剛櫟

7

路線2　台大校園
校園植物與人文自然巡禮
Plants in Literature: Walk Through the Campus Grounds of National Taiwan University

Nestled within the heart of Taipei, National Taiwan University (NTU) contains a grand and spacious sanctuary where nature and academia come together in perfect accord. Across its expansive 111-hectare campus, NTU reveals a landscape rich with history, lush greenery, and a thoughtfully preserved ecosystem. This tranquil haven invites visitors to take their time wandering among the elegant buildings, to admire the rare plants, and to experience a space that exudes quiet inspiration.

Zhoushan Road: A Gentle Prelude to NTU's Tranquility

Beginning at Gongguan MRT Station, the enchanting avenue Zhoushan Road leads visitors into NTU shaded by golden rain trees, cottonwoods, and Javanese bishopwood trees. This verdant corridor changes through the seasons, offering an evolving palette of colors and textures that welcomes visitors into NTU's peaceful world. The soft dappled light, gentle breezes, and vibrant foliage prepare the senses for the beauty that lies within the campus itself.

Liugong Pool: A Living Tribute to Taipei's Ecological Past

Just off Zhoushan Road near the NTU Life Sciences Center,

Liugong Pool—often called the NTU Ecological Pond—stands as a testament to Taipei's natural heritage. Once a saline lake surrounded by wetlands, Liugong Pool was restored in 2003 to recreate a rich habitat for native species. Now encircled by buttonbush, Warburg willows, and pongame oiltrees, the pond's surface gently reflects its lush surroundings. A series of winding paths invites visitors to explore further, as the pond's natural filtration system fosters an abundant ecosystem, where water birds, butterflies, and aquatic plants thrive. This sanctuary offers a serene retreat and a glimpse into the Taipei of centuries past.

Fu Garden: A Harmony of History and Natural Beauty

A short distance from the main NTU gate lies Fu Garden, a cultural treasure intertwined with botanical richness. Originally a botanical specimen garden from Taiwan's colonial era, Fu Garden was later dedicated to former NTU president Fu Ssu-nien. The garden's pathways, inspired by classical Greek architecture, lead visitors to Ssu-nien Hall, where sixteen grand Doric columns evoke the dignified architecture of the Parthenon. Amid the tall Alexandra palms, fan palms, and ancient strangler figs, the garden's serene beauty pays homage to the enduring union of knowledge and nature. Visitors may encounter the vibrant Taiwan blue magpie, the crested goshawk, and other native species, as well as peaceful ponds encircled by verdant greenery—an invitation to pause and savor the interplay of nature and history.

Embracing NTU's Timeless Landscape

NTU's campus is a welcoming oasis for those drawn to the artful blend of nature and academia. From the seasonal transformation of Zhoushan Road to the reflective stillness of Rukong Pond and the storied splendor of Fu Garden, NTU offers an inspiring escape from city life. Here, the rhythms of flora, fauna, and thoughtful architecture weave a living story, inviting visitors to explore and find peace within. This timeless landscape, where history, ecology, and intellectual pursuit flourish side by side, offers a profound experience—one that captures the essence of harmony and quiet beauty at the heart of Taipei.

Transportation

NTU is conveniently located near Gongguan MRT Station on the Green Line. Rukong Pond is a short 500-meter walk from Exit 2 along Zhoushan Road to the Rukong Pond. Fu Garden is a take a three-minute walk from Exit 3. Additionally, the university is accessible by bus and bike-sharing services, making it easy for visitors to explore the greenery and cultural landmarks campus.

English Introduction by: 嚴浩文、彭國欣、劉驊、賴彥瑜

臺大校總區將近 111 公頃，（網路上「臺大總校區位於臺北盆地南緣蟾蜍山山腳，西北面向觀音山，北眺大屯山，東背拇指山，占地約 27 公頃」是不正確的。）植物種類繁多，我根據最近十年來多次導覽的紀錄，重新踏勘修訂，以下是公館捷運 2 號出口沿舟山路，經鹿鳴堂到瑠公池（臺大生態池）約 500 公尺沿途，以及傅園裡的植物。有些珍貴植物，如傅園裡的「臺灣土肉桂」已不見了（給盜採了嗎？）。生態池的「過山香」也消失了，池中許多水生植物也沒了，改種外來植物落羽杉，令人浩歎。

▲ 臺大生態池旁消失了的「過山香」Taiwan Wampee，附上照片以供憑弔。

🐾 台大校園

　　台灣大學成立於 1928 年，校總區佔地 110.76 公頃，除日治時期保存下來的優雅建築外，草木蔥蘢，還有池塘、溼地、農場等，擁有豐富的自然生態資源。

　　台大正門右邊是傅園，原本是日治時代台北帝大的熱帶植物標本園，收集台灣與南洋的熱帶植物栽植於園中，當時熱帶植物標本園的範圍包括現今台大大一女生宿舍及公館捷運站部分現址。

🍃 舟山路（公館捷運 2 號出口）沿途植栽

木棉樹 (*Bombax Ceiba*) Cotton Tree、茄苳/重陽木 Javanese Bishopwood、島榕 Twiggy Fig、台灣欒樹 (*Koelreuteria Formosana*) Taiwan Golden Rain Tree、苦楝 (*Melia azedarach*) Chinaberry、福木 (*Garcinia Subelliptica*)、血桐 Blush Macaranga/ David's Heart、銀杏 (Ginkgo)、石楠 (*Photinia*)、金

露花 (*Duranta repens*) Golden Dewdrop、（吳濁流的《台灣連翹》）、車前草 (*Plantago Major*) Plantain、流蘇 (*Chionanthus retusus*) Chinese Fringe Tree、構樹 Paper Mulberry、桑 Mulberry、姑婆芋 Giant Elephant's Ear、紫薇 Crepe Myrtle、合果芋 Arrowhead Plant/ Arrowhead Vine、楓香 Formosan Sweet Gum、樟樹 Camphor Tree、臺灣赤楠 Taiwan Syzygium、白千層 Weeping Paperbark、崖薑蕨 (*Aglaomorpha coronans*)、兔腳蕨 Hare's Foot Fern、銀樺 Silky Oak、垂榕/白榕 (*Ficus benjamina*)、肯氏蒲桃 Jambolan、雀榕 Deciduous Fig、大葉雀榕 Large-leaf Deciduous Fig、月橘/七里香 Common Jasmine Orange (*Murraya paniculata*)、緬梔 Frangipani、梔子 Gardenia、阿勃勒 Golden Shower Tree、穗花棋盤腳 (*Barringtonia racemosa*) Powder-puff Tree。

瑠公池（臺大生態池）

台北曾經是半鹹水湖及沼澤溼地，所以台大校園至今仍可看到許多水濱植物；諸如水柳 Warburg Willow、風箱樹 Buttonbush (*Cephalanthus tetrandrus*)、水黃皮 Pongame Oiltree、穗花棋盤腳 Powder-puff Tree、欖仁樹 Indian Almond 等。

▲ 夏天夜間開花的穗花棋盤腳 (*Barringtonia racemosa*) Powder-puff Tree（蘇恆隆 攝）

瑠公池 (臺大生態池)，位於舟山路台大生命科學館左方的農場旁，是臺大瑠公圳復原計畫的第一期工程，做為該計畫的水源源頭，於 2003 年 11 月完成。第一期工程包括生態池區、舊圳道區、新設湧泉及水道區、水圳淨化區、瑠公橋、眺望平臺及休憩步道空間等，並栽植數十種水生植物於水源池中及周遭。

瑠公圳在臺大校區內是屬於大安支線的一部分，經過校園內的農場、舟山路、小椰林道及醉月湖。生態池水源主要來自隔壁的生命科學館。

🌿 生態池及周遭的植栽

紙莎草 Papyrus、輪傘莎草 Umbrella Sedge、水柳 Warburg Willow、穗花棋盤腳 Powder-puff Tree、野薑花 White Ginger Lily、馬纓丹 Lantana、緬梔 Frangipani、美人蕉 Canna Lily、月桃 Shell Ginger、曼陀羅 Thorn Apple、烏桕 (*Sapium Sebiferum*) Chinese Tallow Tree、天堂鳥 Bird of Paradise、射干 (*Iris domestica*) Leopard Lily、蜘蛛蘭 Spider Lily、落羽杉 Bald Cypress、蘆葦 Reed、春不老 Ardisia、長穗木 Nettleleaf Velvetberry、石竹 Rainbow Pink/China Pink、無患子 Soapberry。

👣 傅園

1949 年傅斯年先生接任台大第四任校長，1950 年 12 月 20 日辭世。傅校長是著名學者、教育家、五四運動的領袖人物，在動盪不安的時代，維持台大校園內的自由學風，保護師生不受政治干擾，為台大奠定重要的發展基礎。傅校長辭世後，為紀念他對台大的貢獻，各界與傅夫人討論後，決定將傅校長骨灰遷入，1951 年 12 月斯年堂完成，熱帶植物標本園更名為「傅園」。

🌿 傅園周遭的植栽

傅園入口左側兩棵大葉桉（尤加利）*Eucalyptus Robusta* 樹幹上都有雀榕 Deciduous Fig 附生，小圓拱門上爬滿薜荔 Climbing Fig，傅園裡面的熱帶植物有：十字葉蒲瓜樹 Mexican Calabash、穗花棋盤腳 Powder-puff Tree、朴樹 (*Celtis sinensis*) Chinese hackberry、樹杞 Siebolo's Ardisia、亞歷山大椰子 Alexander Palm、大王椰子 Royal Palm、槭葉翅子木 Bayur Tree、大頭茶 Taiwan Gordonia、銀葉樹 Looking-Glass Mangrove、鐵冬青 Kurogane Holly、台灣海棗 Mountain Date Palm、中東海棗 Date Palm、蒲葵 Chinese Fan Palm、旅人蕉 Traveler's Palm、文珠蘭 Poison Bulb、台東蘇鐵 Taitung Cycas、闊葉榕 (高山榕，*Ficus altissima*)、圓果榕 *Ficus globosa*、馬纓丹 *Lantana camara*、九芎 Taiwan Crepe Myrtle、第倫桃 *Dillenia indica* 等，其中十字葉蒲瓜、槭葉翅子木較為罕見。

👣 傅園的建築

傅園的園道與建築設計，仿希臘的帕森農神殿 (Parthenon)。帕森農神殿從入口衛門 (Acropolis) 進入後，路徑蜿蜒，最後才得見神殿正面，隱喻追求學問有許多曲折，峯迴路轉，才得見真章。

斯年堂即是埋放傅斯年骨灰之處，也是仿造帕森農神殿的比例和建築語彙，有十六根多利克柱式 (Doric Order) 圓柱圍繞，柱式沉穩雄壯，只有柱頭與柱身，沒有柱基。柱身有凹槽 (flute)，柱頭是一塊方形頂板，上方是楣樑與飾帶。希臘文明崇尚自由與邏輯，這些建築特色，也反映了傅校長的個性剛直，以及嚴謹、開放的治學態度。斯年堂正中為長方形、高出地表，莊嚴隆重的「傅校長斯年之墓」。

▲ 風箱樹 (*Cephalanthus tetrandrus*) Buttonbush（陳文彬 攝）

　　傅校長斯年之墓前方樹立一座方尖碑 (obelisk)，下大上小，頂為方錐形，是埃及古代象徵太陽的錐形石碑，也代表重要的世界古文明埃及文化。（參考《臺大校訊第 752 期》〈傅園風華再現〉）

台大校園鳥類

紅冠水雞 (*Gallinula chloropus*) Common Moorhen
白腹秧雞 (*Amaurornis phoenicurus chinensis*) White-breasted Waterhen
夜鷺 (*Nycticorax nycticorax*) Black-crowned Night-heron
黑冠麻鷺 (*Gorsachius melanolophus*) Malayan Night Heron
小白鷺 (*Egretta garzetta*) Little Egret
五色鳥 (*Psilopogon nuchalis*) Taiwan Barbet
白鶺鴒 (*Motacilla alba*) White Wagtail

小彎嘴畫眉 (*Pomatorhinus musicus*) Taiwan Scimitar Babbler

領角鴞 (*Otus lettia*) Collared Scops Owl

白頭翁 (*Pycnonotus sinensis*) Chinese Bulbul/Light-Vented Bulbul

家八哥 (*Acridotheres tristis*) Common Myna 入侵種

鵲鴝 (*Copsychus saularis*) Oriental Magpie-robin 外來種

灰頭椋鳥 (*Sturnia malabarica*) Chestnut-tailed Starling 外來種

黑領椋鳥 (*Gracupica nigricollis*) Black-collared Starling 外來種

紅嘴黑鵯 (*Hypsipetes leucocephalus*) Black Bulbul

綠繡眼 (*Zosterops simplex*) Swinhoe's White-eye

珠頸斑鳩 (*Spilopelia chinensis*) Spotted Dove

紅鳩 (*Streptopelia tranquebarica*) Red Collared Dove/Red Turtle Dove

◎**哺乳類**　最常見的哺乳類是赤腹松鼠及傍晚時飛翔校園上空捕食昆蟲的東亞家蝠。

◎**兩棲類及爬蟲類**　黑眶蟾蜍、貢德氏赤蛙和斑龜；生態池常見在岩石上做日光浴的是紅耳泥龜（巴西龜）。最常見的爬蟲是黃口攀蜥。

▲ 紅嘴黑鵯（張雅雯 攝）　　　▲ 夜鷺（蘇恆隆 攝）

導覽地圖

水柳・風箱樹・水黃皮・欖仁樹・紙莎草・輪傘莎草・水柳・穗花棋盤腳・野薑花・馬纓丹・緬梔・美人蕉・月桃・曼陀羅・烏柏・天堂鳥・射干・蜘蛛蘭・落羽杉・蘆葦・春不老・長穗木・石竹・無患子

瑠公池

傅園入口：大葉桉(尤加利)
傅園內：十字葉蒲瓜樹・穗花棋盤腳・大王椰子・城葉翅子木・大花紫薇・雀榕・薜荔
杞・亞歷山大蒲瓜樹・樸樹・樹頭菜・鋸葉樹・鐵冬青・台灣海棗・中東海棗・蒲葵・旅人蕉・文珠蘭・台東蘇鐵・榕・山格・圓果格・馬纓丹・九芎・第倫桃

椰林大道

小椰林道

生命科學館

蝶樹道

鹿鳴堂

銘傳國小

台大正門

傅園

新生南路三段

舟山路

基隆路四段

羅斯福路四段

書林書店

捷運公館站 出口2

木棉樹・茄苳・重陽木・台灣欒樹・苦楝・福木・血桐・流蘇・構樹・銀杏・桑・石楠・金楠・姑婆芋・臺灣赤楠・紫薇・車前草・楓香・樟樹・銀樺・垂榕・白千層・合果芋・兔腳蕨・銀樺・垂榕(白榕)・青氏崖薑蕨・雀榕・大葉雀榕・月橘・七里香・楠桃・梔子・阿勃勒・穗花棋盤腳

17

路線3 溫州社區 / 殷海光故居
社區自然資源與人文記憶
Meander Down the Historic and Cultural Walk of Taipei's Wenzhou Community

  The Wenzhou Community Walk (溫州社區自然步道) covers a square section of Taipei City bounded by Section 3 of Xinsheng South Road (新生南路三段), Section 1 of Heping East Road (和平東路一段), Taishun Street (泰順街), and Section 1 of Xinhai Road (辛亥路一段). Originally a housing complex for National Taiwan University faculty, today its richness lies in lushness of the greenery found there and the vibrancy of its cultural, intellectual history. Wistaria Tea House, the Tai Jingnong House, the Grand Courtyard, and the Yin Hai-Kuang House are all historic landmarks and heritage buildings within this area. If you appreciate Taiwan's journey to becoming a democratic society freedom of speech, a visit here offers a glimpse into the efforts of past intellectuals who helped shape its modern identity.

  Starting from the entrance of the Wistaria Tea House across from Long-An Elementary School, one can walk down Lane 16, Section 3, Xinsheng South Road and arrive at the Tai Jingnong House at the end of the lane. To reach the Grand Courtyard, you can walk down Lane 18 of Wenzhou Street and turn left at Lane 248 of Heping East Road Section 1. Wenzhou Street also leads to another landmark: The Yin Hai-Kuang House is at Alley 16, Lane 18 of Wenzhou Street, while at the end of Lane 18 sits Taishun Park.

👣 Wistaria Tea House（紫藤廬）

No. 1, Lane 16, Sec. 3, Xinsheng South Road. (新生南路三段16巷1號)

　　The Wistaria Tea House, located in Taipei's Da'an District, is a Japanese-style building infused with Daoist influences. In the 1950s, it was the official residence of Chou Te-Wei, the Director-General of the Customs Administration at that time. Chou transformed the residence into a cultural salon, regularly hosting gatherings of liberal intellectuals; Yin Hai-Kuang, Chang Fo-Chuan, Hsu Dao-Lin, Hsia Tao-Ping, and Yin Chung-Jung were all frequent guests. In 1981, the site was transformed into the Wistaria Tea House, becoming a gathering spot for the arts community and non-KMT political advocates. Wistaria Tea House preserves cultural memories from the 1980s to the present day. Its courtyard features a nearly century-old wisteria vine, which was designated a municipal historic landmark in 1997.

👣 Tai Jingnong House（臺靜農故居）

No. 25, Wenzhou Street (溫州街 25 號)

　　This site is the former residence of Tai Jingnong, a renowned calligrapher and scholar of Chinese classics. It has been designated as a heritage site by the Taipei City Department of Cultural Affairs.

👣 Grand Courtyard（大院子）

No. 10, Lane 248, Section 1, Heping East Rd. (和平東路一段248巷10號)

　　Constructed in 1931, the Grand Courtyard is a historic building that originally served as a dormitory for National Taiwan University staff. After a fire in 2013, the site was restored and reopened under the name "Grand Courtyard," now functioning as a cultural venue and restaurant.

👣 Yin Hai-Kuang House (殷海光故居)

No. 1-1, Alley 16, Lane 18, Wenzhou Street (溫州街18巷16弄1之1號)

    Yin Hai-Kuang was a professor in the Department of Philosophy at National Taiwan University. Known for his fearless opposition to authoritarianism, critique of political issues, and advocacy for freedom of speech, he was a pioneer of liberalism in Taiwan. The Yin Hai-Kuang House, designated as a municipal heritage site, preserves and showcases many significant artifacts of his life while standing as a testament to an exemplary intellectual's dedication to the democratic movement during the 1950s. Aside from the house's historic connection to Yin's unwavering dedication to democracy, its courtyard boasts a variety of lush plants including a prominent breadfruit tree.

👣 Taishun Park (泰順公園)

No. 25, Taishun Street (泰順街 25 號)

    Tai Shun Park hosts a plethora of native wildlife, including a number of littoral and riparian vegetation. You can enjoy views of Indian Almond Trees (欖仁樹), Pongam Oiltrees (水黃皮), Decidous Figs (雀榕) and Large-leaf Decidous Figs (大葉雀榕) and more. Remember to stop by as you pass through the Wenzhou Community!

    End your walk at Taishun Park, where the vivid greenery and thriving ecosystem seem almost eternal, much like the enduring legacy of Wenzhou Community's past residents. Their contributions continue to inspire and enrich the lives of Taiwanese people today.

English Introduction by: Lorraine McShea、Kyle Rice、王裕忠、彭心玗

　　溫州社區自然步道是以台北市新生南路三段，和平東路一段，泰順街和辛亥路一段這四條道路所圍出的區域為範圍。此區為台大教授的宿舍群，植栽豐富，處處濃綠青翠，充滿濃厚的人文氣息。其中紫藤廬、臺靜農故居、大院子、殷海光故居皆是古蹟或歷史建築。

　　由龍安國小對面紫藤廬門口出發，沿著新生南路三段 16 巷前行，巷底即臺靜農故居。沿溫州街 18 巷與和平東路一段 248 巷交會處左轉可抵大院子；溫州街 18 巷 16 弄有殷海光故居、18 巷底有泰順公園。

紫藤廬 Wistaria Tea House（新生南路三段 16 巷 1 號）

　　位於台北市大安區的和洋風格混合的日式建築，是 1950 年代海關關務署署長周德偉的官舍，他將官舍作為文化沙龍，定期約集自由派學者殷海光、張佛泉、徐道鄰、夏道平、尹仲容等聚會。1981 年改作紫藤廬茶館，成為藝文界與黨外人士交流的地方，烙印著八〇年代至今的文化記憶。紫藤廬庭院中有株幾近百年的紫藤（Wisteria），1997 年列為市定古蹟。

- 李慈銘《越縵堂日記》中有一則：「紫薇、芭蕉、紫豆乃余之三友。紫薇久花，離離散紅；芭蕉展葉，綠滿窗戶；紫豆一叢，作花甚繁。」紫豆即紫藤廬名稱由來的紫藤。

臺靜農故居 Tai Jingnong House（溫州街 25 號）

　　國學大師、書法家、臺靜農教授故居，台北市文化局登錄紀念建築。

👣 大院子 Grand Courtyard （和平東路一段 248 巷 10 號）

前身為台大宿舍的歷史建物，建於日治昭和 6 年（1931）2013 年遭祝融之災，修復完成後以『大院子』為名作為藝文場所及餐廳對外營業。

👣 殷海光故居 Yin Hai-Kuang House （溫州街 18 巷 16 弄 1 之 1 號）

殷海光先生任教台大哲學系，勇於對抗威權、批評時政，提倡言論自由，是自由主義的先鋒。故居為市定古蹟，保存展示殷海光先生重要的文物，見證五〇年代知識份子參與民主運動之痕跡。

故居門外牆上爬滿薜荔 (Climbing Fig)，巷口有俗稱雞蛋花的「緬梔」(Frangipani)，庭院內植栽豐富，並有一巨大的麵包樹 (Breadfruit Tree)。本書〈花言樹語〉部分介紹了麵包樹引發的《叛艦喋血記》（*Mutiny on the Bounty*）；緬梔英文為何稱為 Frangipani？古今文學中的薜荔 (Climbing Fig) 與愛玉名稱的由來。

- 薜荔 (*Ficus pumila*) Climbing Ficus，Climbing Fig

紫藤廬溫州街 18 巷牆外，整面牆爬滿了薜荔。薜荔為桑科榕屬，是愛玉的兄弟，果實為隱花果。昆蟲進入果實之凹洞，吸取花蜜為它傳粉。薜荔是溫州社區很珍貴的資源，提供了難得的綠色景觀。但鄰里有人認為是雜草，就把它拔除。天生我材必有用，萬物都有它的作用。二千多年前《楚辭》就出現對薜荔的詠唱：「若有人兮山之阿，被薜荔兮帶女蘿，既含睇兮又宜笑，子慕予兮善窈窕。」（她彷若立於山阿，披著薜荔，繫著女蘿，靦腆脈脈地笑著，戀慕地望著我，體態如此優雅。）

溫州社區 / 殷海光故居

▲ 殷海光故居 牆上爬滿了薜荔（張雅雯 攝）

👣 泰順公園（Taishun Park）

在這個社區小公園裡可以看到一些典型的水濱植物 (Littoral and Riparian Vegetation)：欖仁 (Indian Almond)、水黃皮 (Pongam Oiltree)；附近也有雀榕 (Decidous Fig) 與大葉雀榕 (Large-leaf Decidous Fig) 及纏勒現象 (strangling)。

🌿 其他社區可見之植物

Other common plants in the community: 日日春 / 長春花 (*Catharanthus roseus*/*Vinca rosea*) Rosy Periwinkle；台灣欒樹 Taiwan Goldenrain Tree、樟樹 Camphor Tree、木麻黃 Casuarina/Beefwood/Australian Pine、檳榔樹 Betel Palm、大王椰子 Royal Palm、亞歷山大椰子 (*Archontophoenix alexandrae*) Alexandra Palm、黃椰子 (*Chrysalidocarpus lutescens*) Yellow Palm、蒲葵 Chinese Fan Palm、茄苳樹 Javanese Bishopwood、白千層

Weeping Melaleuca/Paperbark Tree、杉木 China Fir、龍柏 Chinese Juniper、蘇鐵 (鐵樹) Cycas、洋玉蘭 (*Magnolia grandiflora*) Magnolia、玉蘭 White Champak、美人蕉 Canna Lily、粗肋草 Chinese Evergreen/Aglaonema、朱槿/扶桑 Chinese Hibiscus、繡球花 Hydrangea、牽牛花 Morning Glory、夜香木 (夜來香) Night Jasmine/Queen-of-the-night、桂花 Sweet Osmanthus/Sweet Olive、筆筒樹 Brush Pot Tree Fern、秋海棠 Begonia、含羞草 Sensitive Plant、聖誕紅 Poinsettia、烏桕 Chinese Tallow Tree、黑板樹 (*Alstonia scholaris*) Blackboard Tree、榕樹 (*Ficus microcarpa*) Chinese banyan (In Hong Kong, *Ficus microcarpa* is called 細葉榕)、大花紫薇 Queen Crape Myrtle、七里香 / 月橘 Orange Jasmine

▲ 洋玉蘭（引自 陳文彬《新細說台灣原生植物》）

▲ 筆筒樹（引自 陳文彬《新細說台灣原生植物》）

導覽地圖

青田街6巷　青田街7巷　和平東路一段183巷　和平東路一段　青田街7巷

青田街

新生南路二段

青田七六
馬廷英故居

24 銀杏樹

洪炎秋故居
澍林

和平東路一段　和平東路二段

豐年大樓
23 錫蘭橄欖

溫州街18巷

22 欖仁樹

殷海光故居

臺靜農故居

新生南路三段

18　19
茄苳、羊蹄甲

17 麵包樹

20　21
薛荔、楊桃

泰順街

溫州街22巷　和平東路一段268巷

溫州街

辛亥路二段

臺大綜合體育館

建國高架道路

辛亥路一段

大學公園
15 楊梅

霧裡薛圳
16 龍眼

新生南路三段

14 血桐

溫州街52巷

溫州街

臺灣大學

12　13
百香果、洋玉蘭

新生南路三段56巷

羅斯福路三段233巷

10 魚木

8　9
蒜香藤、樹蘭

11 七里香

7
尤加利　全家

新生南路三段86巷

真理堂

書林書店

4　5　6
苦楝樹、白千層、小葉欖仁

1　2　3
琉球女貞、楓香、流蘇

溫州公園

25

路線4 瑠公圳 / 霧裡薛圳
探尋水圳，看見原生水濱植物
Liugongzun & Wulixue Canal: The City's Historic Irrigation System and the Variety of Aquatic Life

Did you know that amid the hustle and bustle of Taipei's Da'an District, you can get a glimpse into the city's historic irrigation system and appreciate the variety of aquatic life in its vicinity? Although much of the Liugong Canal (瑠公圳) was covered as Taiwan transitioned away from being an agricultural society, some segments were preserved and reconstructed on and around National Taiwan University's (NTU) campus. These offer us a window into Taiwan's past and the ways in which this land has nurtured generations.

Liugong Pool (瑠公池)

The Liugong Canal once meandered through what is now the NTU campus. As part of its reconstruction project, an artificial pool was created adjacent to Zhoushan Road has since become a thriving habitat for plants and wildlife. In this rare opportunity to connect with nature in an urban setting if you look closely, you might spot kingfishers flitting about, nightingales perched in bald cypress trees, or red-eared turtles basking on rocks between the reeds.

Liugongzun Memorial Stele (瑠公圳原址碑)

A memorial stele was erected alongside Xingsheng S. Road in

commemoration of the original Liugong Canal. However, later research revealed that this site is actually the former location of the Wulixue Canal (霧裡薛圳), sparking debate on the history of Taipei's irrigation system.

During the Qing era, Chinese immigrants arrived in Taiwan to cultivate farmland, but their progress was hindered by ack of water. Guo Xiliu (郭錫瑠), one of these immigrants, worked tirelessly to secure a water source by constructing a canal, which was later named "Liugong Canal" in his honor. Despite numerous challenges, he succeeded in channeling water from the Xindian River to central Taipei, ultimately irrigating over 2,000 hectares of farmland.

Xun-Ji and Wulixue Canal Reconstruction Area (洵跡、霧裡薛圳景觀區)

On the west side of Xingsheng South Road, you'll find two reconstructed sites dedicated to the Wulixue Canal. The Xun-Ji heritage site displays artifacts used in early canal construction, including gabions that fortified shorelines and modified ceramic water urns functioning as primitive concrete conduits.

These exhibits showcase the ingenuity of earlier generations, who overcame hardships with limited resources. In the Wulixue Canal Reconstruction Area, a small canal winds through the Wenzhou Street neighborhood.

The Wulixue Canal flowed through the Guting and Wanhua areas of Taipei and converged with the Liugong Canal in Da'an District.

During the Japanese colonial period, they were consolidated into the Liugongzun Irrigation System, which sparked controversy about their respective origins.

Come and drink in the essence of the Liugong Canal! This restored area not only adds freshness to the city landscape, but also reminds us of the resilience and resourcefulness of past inhabitants, and how nature connects us throughout history.

English Introduction by: Lorraine McShea、Kyle Rice、王裕忠、彭心玨

瑠公池（台大生態池）

台北曾經是半鹹水湖及沼澤溼地，所以台大校園至今仍可看到許多水濱植物；諸如水柳 Warburg Willow、水黃皮 Pongame Oiltree、穗花棋盤腳 Powder-puff Tree、欖仁樹 Indian Almond 等。

瑠公池（台大生態池），位於舟山路台大生命科學館左方的農場旁，是臺大瑠公圳復原計畫的第一期工程，於 2003 年 11 月完成，並栽植數十種水生植物於水源池中及周遭，水源主要來自隔壁地下水層較高的生科館及臺大農場的地下水井。

生命科學館的植栽

大葉雀榕 Large-leaf Decidous Fig、雀榕 Decidous Fig、蓮霧 Jambu、銀樺 Silky Oak

台大生態池的植栽

水蘊草 Large-flowered Waterweed、滿江紅 Mosquitofern/Water Velvet、槐葉萍 Floating Fern、布袋蓮 Water Hyacinth、水芙蓉 / 大萍 Water Cabbage、紙莎草 Papyrus、輪傘莎草 Umbrella

Sedge、水蠟燭/香蒲 Bulrush、水柳 Warburg Willow、穗花棋盤腳 Powder-puff Tree、野薑花 Butterfly Ginger Lily、馬纓丹 Lantana、緬梔 Frangipani、月桃 Shell Ginger、曼陀羅 Thorn Apple、烏桕 Chinese Tallow Tree、天堂鳥 Bird of Paradise、射干 Leopard Lily、蜘蛛蘭 Spider Lily、落羽杉 Bald Cypress、蘆葦 Reed、春不老 Ardisa、長穗木 Nettleleaf Velvetberry、石竹 Rainbow Pink/China Pink、無患子 Soapberry。

台大生態池的動物

魚類：吳郭魚、草魚等；鳥類：翠鳥、夜鷺、白腹秧雞、紅冠水雞、蒼鷺、五色鳥、鷺鷥等；兩棲類：貢德氏赤蛙等；爬蟲類：巴西龜、斑龜等。生態池位於臺大農場旁，有一些原本就在農場內的生物，像是福壽螺等，也會進入生態池內。許多民眾也將水族動物、巴西龜放生到池內，往往干擾破壞生態池環境。

瑠公圳ㄗㄨㄣˋ

*(以下瑠公圳之介紹係根據網路資料濃縮整理)

1736 年（乾隆元年）郭錫瑠先生從彰化北上，在現台北松山中崙（興雅庄）一帶開墾。由於當時附近柴頭埤（現信義區靠山邊一帶）淤積，無法灌溉大部份的農田。郭錫瑠眼看大片土地因缺水無法種水稻，覺得非常可惜，便決心尋找新水源。他到附近沿溪探勘，發現新店溪上游青潭附近水源豐沛，河床又高，認為只要沿新店溪畔開鑿水圳，經大坪林、景美等地區，就可以解決台北盆地的灌溉問題。

但要順利將水引入興雅庄內，最大的困難就在於如何將圳水

引過 90 多公尺寬的景美（霧裡薛）溪。

郭錫瑠設計一種木製引水槽，架在溪上，引圳水過溪，這種引水槽稱為「木梘」（景美的台語叫「梘尾」，就是木梘的那一頭）。自從有了木梘之後，民眾就走木梘來代替坐船渡河，因此沒幾年，木梘就損毀無法使用。於是郭錫瑠想辦法解決，他訂購大批水缸，將水缸去底接成管線，引圳水過景美溪，才恢復供水。瑠公圳灌溉的農田從大坪林、景美，直到台北市地區，將近兩千多頃。瑠公圳的大安支線一部分經過臺大農場、舟山路、小椰林道及醉月湖。

★ 註：圳ㄗㄨㄣˋ，指灌溉用的水渠。如：「瑠公圳」、「嘉南大圳」；圳ㄓㄣˋ，指田野間的水溝。如：「深圳」。

引起爭議的新生南路三段 瑠公圳原址碑

在新生南路三段台大校門附近，有一「瑠公圳遺原址」石碑，記載郭錫瑠開拓圳道歷史。新生南路在日治初期有一段人工挖掘的堀川，沿新生南路經霧裡薛圳支圳，到新生北路大排水系統，但與瑠公圳有一些距離。

日治時代將水圳管理由民營改為公營，名稱也合併為「瑠公水利組合」，因此後人一碰到台北圳道，都叫瑠公圳。

台灣師範大學地理系洪致文教授指出，目前台大側門立的「瑠公圳原址」碑，比對古地圖應為清朝「霧裡薛圳」舊址，而非「瑠公圳」。

霧裡薛圳遺址 (1907 年後為瑠公圳第二幹線)

霧裡圳開發比瑠公圳更早（約 1735 年），取景美溪水，穿越景興路，景後街到景美國中，公館蟾蜍山，在 1735 年到 1908 年

之間，霧裡圳與瑠公圳並存。瑠公圳在羅斯福路四段 119 巷向東走，霧裡薛圳是向北走，灌溉古亭、艋舺、大同區一帶。(1908 年以後稱瑠公圳西幹線）

霧裡薛圳在羅斯福路四段 12 巷附近，經羅斯福路三段，到 302 號附近穿越羅斯福路，流向新生南路三段的溫州街。

洵跡（霧裡薛圳遺址）

在新生南路三段 58 號的一處景觀區，取名洵跡。主要係呈現霧裡薛圳、瑠公圳在公館、台大附近昔日灌溉系統的足跡，展示古代生態工法維護圳道的石籠。圳道涵洞所用的水缸，如同現代水泥管。

A、園中植物：朱槿 Hibiscus、藍星花 Shaggy Dwarf Morning-glory、金英花 Golden Thryallis、桔梗蘭 Common Dianella、天門冬 Chinese Asparagus

B、周遭自生植物：虎葛/烏斂莓/五爪龍 Japanese Cayratia Herb、霧水葛 Pouzolzia、三角葉西番蓮 Corkystem Passionflower、五蕊油柑 Mascarene Island Leaf-flower、瑪瑙珠 Twoleaf Nightshade、珊瑚珠 Pigeonberry/Rougeplant

霧裡薛圳九汴頭

汴頭是指圳溝分水用的閘門，九汴頭的「九」是指好多個，不一定是九個，就像九層塔不一定有九層花序，九孔不一定是九個孔。

在新生南路三段 54 巷底，霧裡薛圳在此分為幾條支線。東線穿越台大體育館，灌溉復興南路沿線；中線為主線，向北通向中山區；西線沿羅斯福路通到艋舺。

霧裡薛圳景觀區（大學里）

在九汴頭後方，溫州街 49 巷內，有一處霧裡薛圳景觀復原區，圳水清澈，水中不少游魚及巴西龜。

植物有柳樹 Weeping Willow、桑 Mulberry、文珠蘭 Poison Bulb、桃金孃 Myrtle、姑婆芋 Giant Elephant's Ear、流蘇 Chinese Fringe Tree、構樹 Paper Mulberry、蔓馬櫻丹 Climbing Lantana、番石榴 Guava 等。

周遭還有麵包樹 Breadfruit、龍眼 Longan、木瓜 Papaya、福木 Fukugi Tree、楊梅 Chinese Bayberry、楓香 Sweet Gum 等。

▲ 洵跡一景 展示著石籠與圳道用的水缸（張雅雯攝）

導覽地圖

水蕨、滿江紅、槐葉蘋、布袋蓮、水芙蓉、紙莎草、輪傘莎草、水蠟燭、水柳、穗花棋盤腳、野薑花、馬櫻丹、緬梔、月桃、曼陀羅、烏桕、天堂鳥、射干、蜘蛛蘭、落羽杉、蘆葦不老、長穗木、石竹、無患子

台灣大學

瑠公池（台大生態池）
生命科學館
大葉雀榕、蕉榕
蓮霧、銀樺

園中植物：朱槿、藍星花、金英花、桔梗蘭、天門冬
週邊植物：五爪龍、霧水葛、三角葉西番蓮、五蕊油柑、瑪瑙珠、珊瑚珠

柳樹、桑、文珠蘭、桃金孃、姑婆芋、流蘇、構樹、蔓馬櫻丹、番石榴
週邊植物：麵包樹、龍眼、楊梅、福木、楓香

新月台
瑠公圳紀念碑
網球場

台大綜合體育館
霧裡薛圳
鳳城燒臘店
泗跡
全家超商
臺大書店
大學公園
楊梅

辛亥路一段、辛亥路二段、辛亥路三段
基隆路三段、基隆路四段
新生南路三段
羅斯福路三段、羅斯福路四段
建國高架道
溫州街

路線5　芝山岩 / 北隘門步道
滄海桑田，千萬年岩丘中的秘密
Zhishan Yan—Stories Spanning Millions of Years Found in Sandstone

Entering the Zhishan Yan Nature Trail feels like stepping into a majestic time tunnel, where the natural and cultural history of Zhishan Yan unfolds before you. This small hill located in Shilin, Taipei offers a 3.5-kilometer loop that winds through diverse plant life at different elevations. Hikers may come across fossils and cultural relics along the way, giving a peek into the varied history of the Taipei Basin.

Zhishan Yan got its name from Zhangzhou immigrants, who settling in Shihlin, noticed the resemblance of Zhishan Yan to the hill named "Zhishan" in Zhangzhou, Fujian. As you walk along the path, you can see more of Zhishan Yan's military history: its fortified gates, built by Zhangzhou settlers amid their fierce faction fights with Quanzhou settlers, offer a glimpse into Qing dynasty-era Taiwan. At that time, most Chinese immigrants living in the Shilin area were from Zhangzhou or Quanzhou, and conflicts over resources like water and land were frequent. Originally, the settlers built four gates or entrances to the town—North, South, East, and West—but today, only ruins of the North and West Gates remain.

In addition to its cultural heritage, Zhishan Yan also has a vibrant natural history. The sandstone hill experienced millions of years of weathering, erosion, and sea-level fluctuations, eventually becoming the peak we know today. The hill also boasts a unique range of plant life, including beautiful wetland and coastal plants that have continued to thrive after the drop in sea level. You can even see fossils of sea urchins in the rock formations, showing how the hill was once submerged underwater.

English Introduction by: Lorraine McShea、Kyle Rice、王裕忠、彭心玗

芝山岩為臺北市士林一帶的砂岩小山丘，標高約51.5 當地人又稱之為「圓山仔」。18世紀大量福建漳州移民移居附近的台北八芝蘭（士林），因其小山丘很像中國漳州芝山，故名芝山岩。

芝山岩隘門是1825年所建，傳統聚落往往於險要處設置隘門或堡壘等防禦設施。清代來臺移民因爭奪田地、水源或利益出現衝突時，就各自糾集同祖籍、姓氏或職業的群眾，相互鬥毆，稱為「分類械鬥」(faction fights)。芝山岩隘門是19世紀分類械鬥中，漳州人為防範泉州人進犯所興建。芝山岩之東西南北四隘門，現僅留下北隘門與西隘門。

芝山岩在2千萬年前與台北盆地同是海底沉積之頁岩層及砂岩層 (stratum of sedimentary shale and sandstone)，在芝山岩上可發現古生物貝類化石。在約400萬年前，芝山岩一帶因板塊擠壓的造山運動 (orogeny) 擠出海面。隨後的風化侵蝕，頁岩層逐漸侵蝕，只剩較堅硬的砂岩層。40萬年前，台北盆地因山腳斷層 (Shanchiao fault) 陷落而逐漸形成，芝山岩成為盆地邊緣的小山丘。約1萬1千年前，因海水面上升導致台北盆地逐漸成為一大鹹水湖，芝山岩則成為小孤島，直到湖水退去後形成今日樣貌。芝山岩的地質為古老的大寮層，岩石節理 (joint) 發達，加上長久以來的侵蝕，使得芝山岩擁有許多特殊的地質景觀，包括太陽石、風化窗、洋蔥石、石象等。

因芝山岩曾為鹹水湖中的小島，故可發現山丘上有皮孫木、搭肉刺、魯花樹等海岸植物 (coastal plants) 的現象。加上芝山岩歷經台北淡水湖和沼澤溼地時期，多變的環境使芝山岩有豐富的植物種類。日治時期紀錄芝山岩當地有 400 多種植物及台灣特有種「八芝蘭竹」。因此芝山岩的天然林、蝙蝠洞、石馬、石象、石龍、石頭公及隘門在 1933 年獲臺灣總督府指定為史蹟及天然紀念物。

🍃 文化生態綠園看板及涼亭周遭植物

金腰箭舅 Straggler Daisy/Horseherb、構樹 Paper Mulberry、龍葵 Black Nightshade、瑪瑙珠 Twoleaf Nightshade、福木 Fukugi Tree、金露花 Golden Dewdrop、台灣鱗球花 Taiwan Lepidagathis、朴樹 Chinese Hackberry、五蕊油柑 Mascarene Island Leaf-flower、光蠟樹 Griffith's Ash/Formosan Ash、台灣欒樹 Taiwan Goldenrain Tree、構樹 Paper Mulberry、盤龍木/牛筋藤 Burny Vine、楓香 Sweet Gum、樟樹 Camphor tree、白玉蘭 White Champak、龍眼 Longan、芒果 Mango

密源植物：馬利筋 Tropical Milkweed、咸豐草 Beggarticks/Spanish Needles、馬纓丹 Lantana

🍃 石頭公周遭植物

大葉雀榕 Large-leaf Decidous Fig、雀榕 Decidous Fig、島榕 Twiggy Fig、朴樹 Chinese Hackberry

🍃 北隘門步道沿途植物

山黃麻 Oriental Trema、杜虹 Beautyberry、糙葉樹 Rough Leaf Tree、鴨腳木/鵝掌柴 Common Schefflera、血桐 Blush

Macaranga/David's Heart、軟毛柿 Woolly-flowered Persimmon、陰香 Indonesian Cinnamon、雞屎樹 Lasianthus (*lasios*, "velvety, hairy", *anthos*, "flower")、虎葛/五爪龍 Japanese Cayratia Herb、血桐 Blush Macaranga/David's Heart、風藤 Kadsura Pepper 青苧麻 (*Boehmeria nivea*) False Nettle、巢蕨 Bird's Nest Fern、稜果榕 (*Ficus septica*) White-veined Fig/Septic Fig、茄苳 Janvanese Bishopwood、紅樓花 Firespike/Cardinal Guard、月桃 Shell Ginger、青剛櫟 Ring-cupped Oak、無患子 Soapberry、洋落葵 (*Anredera cordifolia*) Madeira Vine、葛藤 Kudzu、山棕 Taiwan Sugar Palm、杜英 Woodland Elaeocarpus 姑婆芋 Giant Elephant's Ear、拎樹藤 Dragon-tail Plant、合果芋 Arrowhead Plant/Arrowhead Vine、黃金葛 Golden Pothos；台灣朴樹 / 石朴 Taiwan Hackberry、朴樹 / 沙朴 Chinese Hackberry；大葉楠 Large-leaved Machilus、香楠 Incense Machilus、豬腳楠（紅楠）Common Machilus；九芎 Taiwan Crepe Myrtle、紫薇 Crepe Myrtle

🌿 化石群周遭植物

槲蕨 Gu-sui-bu、杯狀蓋骨碎補 / 兔腳蕨 (*Humata griffithiana*) Rabbit's Foot Fern、雀榕 Decidous Fig、鴨腳木 Common Schefflera

🌿 時間廣場周遭植物

八芝蘭竹 *Bambusa pachinensis* 台灣特有種，1916 年日本植物學家早田文藏 (Hayata) 在士林發現的，士林舊名「八芝蘭」。

九芎 Crepe Myrtle、合果芋 Arrowhead Plant/Arrowhead Vine、珊瑚珠 Pigeonberry/Rougeplant、酸藤 Sour Creeper、蟲屎 / 墨鱗木 *Melanolepis multiglandulosa*

🍃 惠濟宮 / 懷古亭周遭植物

蜀葵 Hollyhock、蒲桃 / 香果 Rose Apple、欖仁 Indian Almond、月橘 Common Jasmine Orange、九重葛 Bougainvillea、梅 Chinese Plum、柚 pomelo

🍃 其他雙子葉植物

腺果藤 *Pisonia aculeata*、皮孫木 Pisonia/Birdlime tree/Bird Catcher Tree、猿尾藤 Bengal Hiptage、刺杜密 Prickly Bridelia、粗糠柴 Red Kamala、扛香藤 Climbing Mallotus、青剛櫟 Ring-cupped Oak、魯花樹 *Oldham Scolopia*、土楠/海南厚殼桂 *Endiandra hainanensis*、大葉釣樟 / 大香葉樹 Large-leaved Lindera、搭肉刺 *Caesalpinia crista*、猿尾藤 Bengal Hiptage、木防己 Queen Coralbead、樹杞 Siebold Ardisia、海桐 Pittosporum/Sticky Seed Tree、台灣石楠 Taiwan Photinia、對面花 Spiny Randia、石苓舅 / 山桔 Malay Glycosmis、長葉苧麻 False Nettle、小葉冷水麻 Rockweed、九節木 *Psychotria rubra*、山埔姜 Fiveleaf Chastetree（掌狀複葉，對生）

🍃 鳥類

白頭翁 Chinese Bulbul、綠繡眼 Swinhoe's White-eye、紅嘴黑鵯 Black Bulbul、五色鳥 Taiwan Barbet、山紅頭 Rufous-capped Babbler、黑枕藍鶲 Black-naped Monarch、小彎嘴畫眉 Taiwan Scimitar Babbler、樹鵲 Grey Treepie

▲ 綠繡眼（沈競辰 攝）

導覽地圖

臺北市立聯合醫院 陽明院區

芝山岩文化生態綠園看板

出發里程

金腰箭舅、構樹、龍葵、瑪瑙珠、福木、金露花、台灣鱗球花、朴樹、五蕊油柑、光蠟樹、龍眼、芒果、台灣欒樹、構樹、榕樹、盤龍木、楓香、樟樹、白玉蘭、馬利筋、大花咸豐草

鳥類

白頭翁、綠繡眼、紅嘴黑鵯、五色鳥、山紅頭、黑枕藍鶲、小彎嘴畫眉

其他雙子葉植物

桫欏、杯狀蓋骨碎補、雀榕、鴨腳木

腺果藤、皮孫木、猿尾藤、刺杜密、粗糠柴、杠香藤、青剛櫟、魯花樹、土楠、大葉釣樟、搭肉刺、猿尾藤、木防己、樹杞、海桐、台灣石楠、對面花、石苓舅、長葉空廉、小葉冷水麻、九節木、山埔姜

石頭公（聖佑宮）

大葉雀榕、雀榕、鳥榕、朴樹

化石群

惠濟宮/懷古亭

北隘門步道

時間廣場

蜀葵、蒲桃、欖仁、月橘、九重葛、梅、柚

山黃麻、杜虹、糙葉樹、大葉雀榕、鴨腳木、陰香、血桐、軟毛柿、姑婆芋、拎樹藤、五爪龍、合果芋、黃金葛、雞屎樹、九芎、朴樹、大葉楠、香楠、青苧麻、巢蕨、稜果榕、茄苳、紅楠、桃花、青剛櫟、無患子、洋落葵、葛藤、山棕、杜英、八芝蘭竹

八芝蘭竹、九芎、合果芋、珊瑚珠、酸藤、蟲屎

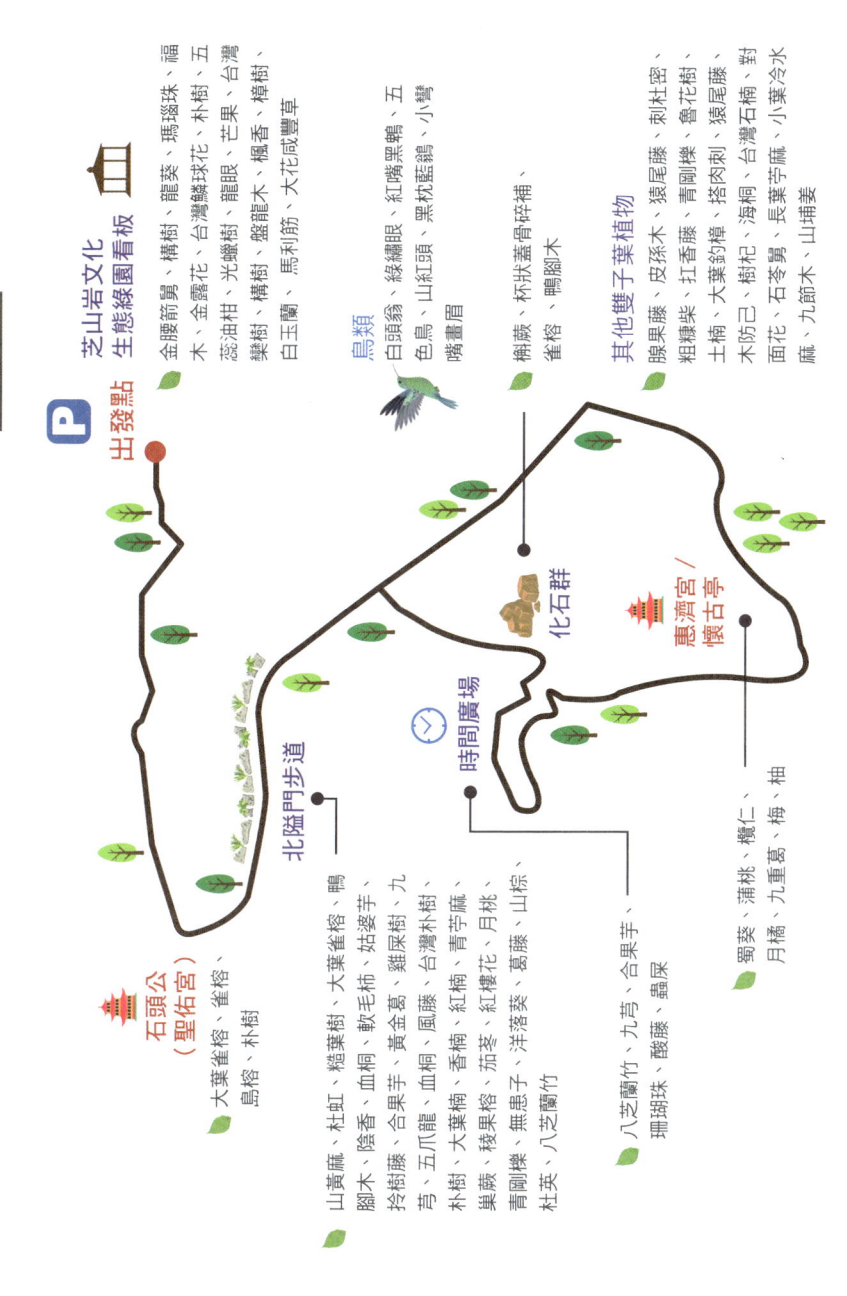

39

路線6　仙跡岩

鬧市仙居的生態人文探索
Xianji Rock Trail: Flora, Fauna, and Literature

Xianji Rock (仙跡岩), located on Xizikou Mountain (Jingmei Mountain) in Wenshan District, Taipei, is a fascinating cultural and natural landmark. At an elevation of around 100 meters, it features a massive exposed rock with a footprint-shaped depression, believed to have been left by the immortal Lü Dongbin. A temple dedicated to Lü Dongbin stands nearby, adding a spiritual dimension to the site.

The trail begins at the Xianji Rock Archway (No. 1, Lane 243, Jingxing Road, Jingmei). The front ground of Zhishan Community Learning Center near the archway can serve as a meeting point. Along the 2 or 3 kilometer round-trip path, hikers can visit notable sites like Zifan Temple, Cishan Pavilion, and Xianji Rock Temple. The trail is surrounded by lush greenery, including over 60 plant species such as Taiwan acacia, ferns, and climbing vines, offering a hike rich in both natural beauty and cultural significance.

至善園 (Zhishan Community Learning Center)

Zhishan Community Learning Center is the trailhead of Xianji Rock Trail where pathways lead you past an impressive variety of plants: sweet olive whose fragrance is so pleasant; Giant Elephant's Ear with large, heart-shaped leaves up to a meter in length; and Javanese Bishopwood that produces small, round, golden-yellow fruits.

紫範宮 (Zhifan Temple)

Along the trail, you'll come across vibrant blooms like the brilliant red Firespike, which stands out beautifully against the lush greenery, along with the unique Thorn Apple and resilient King's Fig. As you continue, Zhifan Temple appears on your right, framed by native plants such as the captivating Chinese Pothos, known for its elegant leaves connecting stalk to leaf blade. The Xiān Jì Yán Trail is an ideal escape from Taipei's urban buzz, winding through a peaceful landscape that invites relaxation. This scenic path offers a refreshing retreat, immersing you in the tranquil beauty of Taipei's greenery—a perfect spot to unwind and reconnect with nature.

慈善亭 (Cishan Pavilion)

Leaving Zhifan Temple, the trail continues with lush vegetation on all sides. Alongside common figs and Spanish Needles, you'll find Taiwan Goldenrain Trees, which bloom with striking red flowers in the autumn. Other plants lining the trail include Giant Elephant's Ear, Shell Ginger, Woodsorrel, among others. Before reaching the end of the trail, you can pause at Cishan Pavilion to rest and take in the surroundings. The pavilion offers an ideal spot to catch your breath while enjoying views of Taipei 101 and the cityscape. While you relax, see if you can see the Sweet Gum, Kadsura Pepper, and Paper Mulberry there, and enjoy the bird song serenading you in the background.

仙跡岩廟 (Xianji Yan Temple)

From the Cishan Pavilion, if you continue up the trail, you will reach Xianji Yan Temple. It is said that the immortal Lü Dongbin left his footprints here, so later generations built a temple in his honor. In addition to the Taiwan Goldenrain trees, you can see many other plants in this area, such as the Bird's Nest Fern, which often grows on tree trunks and rock faces. The accumulation of fallen leaves from various tree species near it resembles a bird's nest, which is how it got its name. Other notable plants here include False-nettle, Dense-flowered False-nettle, and Oriental Debregeasia, all of which beautifully embellish the journey's endpoint.

English Introduction by: 林婉菁、林品妤、陳瑟娟、吳佳謙

　　仙跡岩位於台北市文山區溪子口山（景美山），在海拔100公尺左右木造涼亭處有一巨大裸岩，岩石上有凹陷，似人的腳印，傳說是仙人呂洞賓在此留下的足跡，信眾在此建有一呂洞賓廟。

　　仙跡岩步道可由景美景興路243巷1號登山口、仙跡岩牌樓左上方至善園出發，途經紫範宮、慈善亭、仙跡岩廟，來回約兩三公里。沿途可見許多鳥類與台灣早期為製作木炭種植的相思樹，以及蕨類、藤本植物等六七十種植物，以下為這些動植物的中英文名稱。

　　動物類有保育類動物翡翠樹蛙 Green Treefrog、台北樹蛙 Taipei Treefrog。鳥類有樹鵲 Grey Treepie、紅嘴黑鵯 Black Bulbul、白頭翁 Chinese Bulbul、綠繡眼 Swinhoe's White-eye、五色鳥 Taiwan Barbet、山紅頭 Rufous-capped Babbler、黑枕藍鶲 Black-naped Monarch、小彎嘴畫眉 Taiwan Scimitar Babbler、領角鴞 Collared Scops Owl、台灣藍鵲 Taiwan Blue Magpie 等。

🌿 至善園周遭植栽

桂花 (*Osmanthus fragrans*) Sweet Osmanthus/Sweet Olive、含笑 Port Wine Magnolia、姑婆芋 Giant Elephant's Ear、伏石蕨 Little-leaf Lemmaphyllum、紫花酢醬草 Pink Woodsorrel、黃鵪菜 Oriental False Hawksbeard、蓮霧 Jambu、木瓜 Papaya、冇骨消 Taiwan Elderberry、血桐 Blush Macaranga/David's Heart、破布子 Cordia/Fragrant Manjack、山桂花 Maesa、桑 Mulberry、茄苳 Javanese Bishopwood、台灣鱗球花 Taiwan Lepidagathis

🌿 紫範宮周遭植栽

紅樓花 Firespike/Cardinal Guard：屬常綠灌木，高 1-2m，原產中美洲，逸出入侵台灣山林。葉對生寬卵形，枝條直立，常從基部分枝，少側枝，節處膨大。

曼陀羅 Thorn Apple、水冬瓜 Sinoadina/Taiwan Adina、咖啡 Coffee、風藤 Kadsura Pepper、月桃 Shell Ginger、楊梅 Chinese Bayberry、華八仙 Chinese Hydrangea、柚葉藤 Chinese Pothos（單身複葉，葉柄端上有小型的葉翼，連接著前面的葉片，如：柚子、檸檬。Unifoliate compound leaves have a leaf wing at the petiole, such as pomelo and lemon.）、菲律賓榕 King's Fig、青剛櫟 Ring-cupped Oak、白匏子 Turn-in-the-wind、朴樹 Chinese Hackberry、串鼻龍 Gourian Clematis、觀音座蓮 Turnip Fern、燈秤花 Plum-leaved Holly（小枝光滑褐色似秤桿，皮孔似秤點，故名燈秤花。）、山棕 Taiwan Sugar Palm、島榕 Twiggy Fig、拎樹藤 Dragon-tail Plant、穿鞘花 Flower On Sheath

🌿 慈善亭附近植物

楓香 Sweet Gum、風藤 Kadsura Pepper、黃金葛 Golden Pothos、

山黃麻 Oriental Trema、龍眼 Longan、鴨腳木（江某）Common Schefflera、冬青 Holly、水冬瓜 Sinoadina/Taiwan Adina、豬腳楠（紅楠）Common Machilus、山棕 Taiwan Sugar Palm、構樹 Paper Mulberry、含笑花 Port Wine Magnolia、五爪龍 Japanese Cayratia Herb、相思樹 (*Acacia confusa*) Formosa Acacia

🌿 上行到涼亭途中植物

楊梅 Chinese Bayberry、菲律賓榕 King's Fig、姑婆芋 Giant Elephant's Ear、破布烏 *Ehretia dicksonii*、華八仙 Chinese Hydrangea、密花苧麻 Dense-flowered False-nettle、含笑花 Port Wine Magnolia、無患子 Soapberry、月桃 Shell Ginger、島榕 Twiggy Fig、大花咸豐草 Beggarticks/Spanish Needles、車前 Plantain、紫花酢醬草 Pink Woodsorrel、台灣欒樹 Taiwan Goldenrain Tree、穿鞘花 Flower on Sheath、柚 Pomelo、稜果榕 (*Ficus septica*) White-veined Fig/Septic Fig

🌿 仙跡岩廟周遭植物

巢蕨 Bird's Nest Fern、珊瑚珠 Pigeonberry/Rougeplant、無患子 Soapberry、台灣欒樹 Taiwan Goldenrain Tree、長葉苧麻 False-nettle、密花苧麻 Dense-flowered False-nettle、水麻 Oriental Debregeasia

導覽地圖

仙跡岩廟

楊梅
姑婆芋

巢蕨、珊瑚珠、無患子、台灣欒樹、長葉苧麻、密花苧麻、水麻

楊梅、菲律賓榕、姑婆芋、破布烏、華八仙、密花苧麻、含笑花、無患子、月桃、島榕、大花咸豐、紫花酢醬草、台灣欒樹、穿鞘花、柚、稜果榕、車前

構樹

慈善亭

人傑地靈
蓋根抱石

樟樹

相思樹

楓香、風藤、黃金葛、山黃麻、龍眼、鴨腳木（江某）、冬青、水冬瓜、豬腳楠、山棕、構樹、含笑花、五爪龍

紅樓花、曼陀羅、水冬瓜、風藤、月桃、楊梅、咖啡、華八仙、柚葉藤、菲律賓榕、青剛櫟、白匏子、朴樹、串鼻龍、觀音座蓮、燈秤花、山棕、島榕、拎樹藤、穿鞘花

燈秤花

華八仙

紫範宮

至善園

桂花、含笑、姑婆芋、伏石蕨、紫花酢醬草、黃鵪菜、蓮霧、木瓜、苧麻消、血桐、破布子、山桂花、桑、茄苳、台灣鱒球花

景興路243巷

出發點

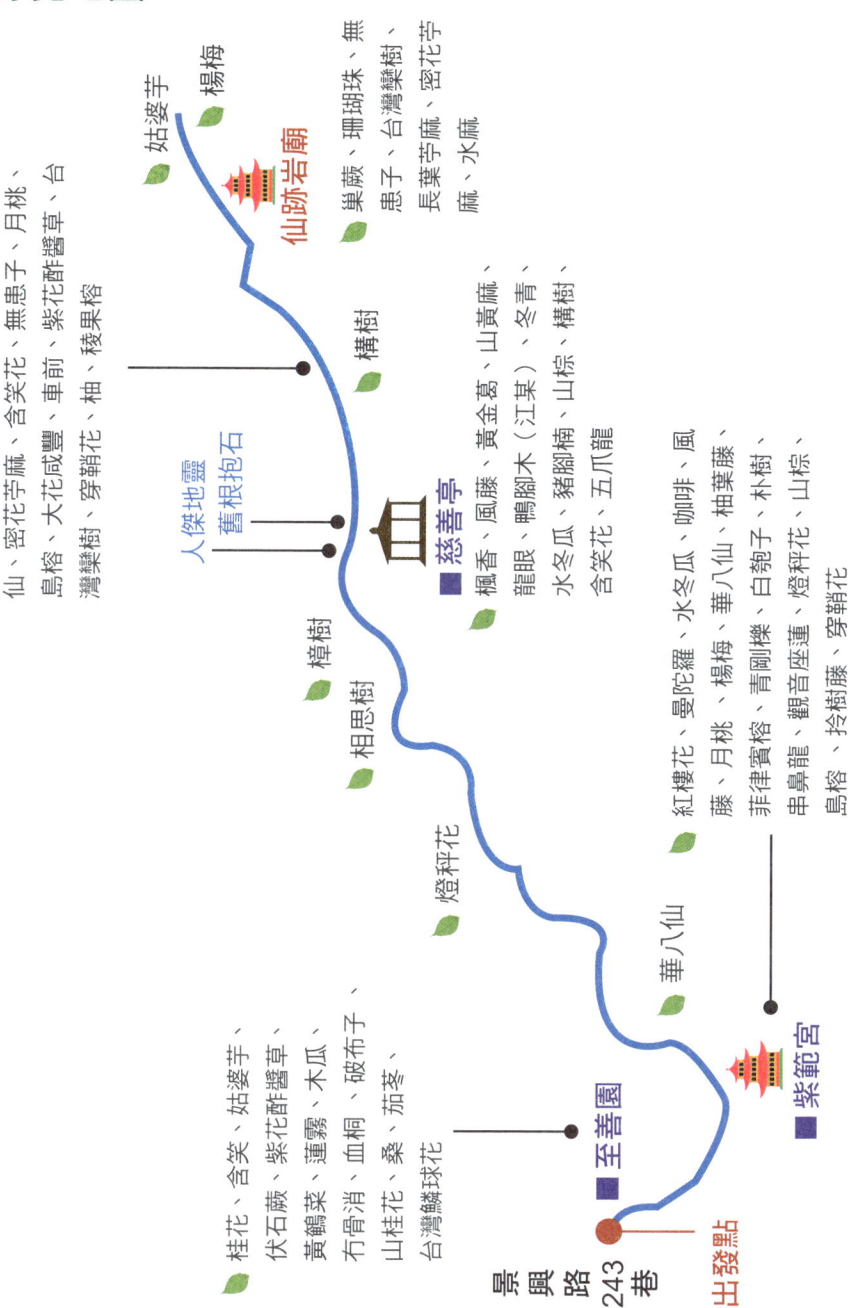

45

路線7 象山

走過侏儸紀活化石林，俯瞰台北
Xiangshan Hiking Trail: Flora, Fauna, and Fiction

Xiangshan (Elephant Mountain), so named for its elephant-head-like silhouette, rises 183 meters above sea level, boasting the highest peak of the Four Beasts Mountains (Sishoushan). The trail crests the hill, and from this vantage point visitors are treated to captivating panoramic views of the Taipei Basin, including iconic landmarks like Taipei 101 and the Taipei World Trade Center.

The 1.5 kilometer trail, meandering above the southeast of the city in Xinyi District, presents a roughly 2-hour sojourn through nature. Along the path, one beholds soaring sheer cliffs, looming sandstone boulders, flourishing plants, and numerous thriving creatures, as well as bask in all parts of Nature's symphony.

The humid, sheltered environment of Xiangshan fosters a perfect treasure trove of ferns, as dozens of species thrive in the shade against the hillsides, between rocks, and clinging to tree trunks along the trail. The richest of these is the luscious Golden Chicken Fern, one of the most prolific species in northern Taiwan. Complementing this vivid tapestry are clusters of ancient tree ferns locally called brush pot trees. Relics from the Jurassic era, they stand as silent sentinels of the mountain, watching over the nature-lovers and photographers treading upon the trail.

How to Get There:

1. Take the Taipei Metro to MRT Xiangshan Station on the Red Line.
2. Leave from Exit 2.
3. Walk toward Zhongqiang Park (about a 15-minute walk from the station).
4. Look for the trailhead at the entrance of the park. The path leading to the trail should be clearly visible.

English Introduction by: 嚴浩文、彭國欣、劉驊、賴彥瑜

象山因外形似象頭而得名，海拔 183 公尺，較虎山為高，是四獸山步道系統中最高點，視野遼闊，臺北 101 大樓、世貿中心等盡在眼底，臺北盆地一覽無遺。

象山位於臺北盆地東南方的信義區，步道約 1.5 公里，全程約需 2 小時。沿途可見陡峭的岩壁與黃褐色砂岩巨石，動植物種類繁多，生態豐富多元。

象山潮濕的環境中蕨類有數十種，有的附生在樹幹上，有的長在岩石、坡地、林下。其中金狗毛蕨數量極多，在北台灣數一數二。此外還有侏儸紀時期就存在的古老蕨類「筆筒樹」成群林立，是賞蕨的好去處。

交通：捷運象山站 2 號出口，往中強公園方向步行，約 15 分鐘抵登山口。

🌱 象山公園周遭植栽 Xiangshan Park

車前 (Chinese) Plantain、苦楝 Chinaberry、落羽杉 Swamp Cypress、九芎 (Taiwan) Crepe Myrtle、通泉草 Japanese Mazus/Asian Mazus、白三葉草 White Clover、水黃皮 Pongame Oiltree

🍃 台北樹蛙棲地周遭植栽
Taipei Tree Frog Sanctuary

咸豐草 Beggarticks/Spanish Needles、野薑花 Butterfly Ginger Lily、月桃 Shell Ginger、野牡丹 Melastoma

大花咸豐草 1978 從琉球引進，作為養蜂的蜜源植物 Spanish Needles were imported into Taiwan in 1978 as a honey plant. Ironically, they were imported not from Spain, but from the nearby Ryukyu Islands (Okinawa).

咸豐草：小白花
大花咸豐草：大白花
鬼針草：無白花

▲ 大花咸豐草（鄭杏倩 繪）

🍃 中強公園周遭植栽 Zhongqiang Park

流蘇 Chinese Fringe Tree、第倫桃 Indian Dillenia、黑板樹 Blackboard Tree

🍃 三犁公園周遭植栽 Sanli Park（信義路 5 段 150 巷 2 號）
(No. 2, Lane 150, Xinyi Road Section 5)

紫花酢漿草 Pink Woodsorrel、酢醬草（黃花）Yellow Woodsorrel、串鼻龍 (*Clematis grata*) Pleasing Clematis、蛇莓 Mock Strawberry/Indian-strawberry、黃鵪菜 Oriental False Hawksbeard

象山

▲ 從象山步道眺望台北一景

- 🌿 **象山入口附近植物 Xiangshan Trailhead**（信義路 5 段 150 巷 22 弄）(Alley 22, Lane 150, Xinyi Road Section 5)
  巢蕨 Bird's Nest Fern

- 🌿 **靈雲宮前周遭植物 In Front of Lingyun Temple**
  木瓜 Papaya (Female)、龍眼 Longan、甘蔗 Sugarcane、柚 Pomelo、芒果 Mango

- 🌿 **步道沿途植物（往六巨石沿途）Along the Trail (Toward the Six Giant Rocks)**
  拎樹藤 Centipede Tongavine/Taro Vine、月橘 Common Jasmine Orange、姑婆芋 Giant Elephant's Ear、洋落葵 (*Anredera*

cordifolia) Madeira Vine、桑 Mulberry、血桐 Blush Macaranga/David's Heart、合果芋 Arrowhead Plant/Arrowhead Vine、構樹 Paper Mulberry、軟毛柿 Woolly-flowered Persimmon、黃金葛 Golden Pothos、華八仙 Chinese Hydrangea、黃梔 (*Gardenia jasminoides*) Cape Jasmine

🌿 瞭望台、攝影平台、永春亭周遭植物 Observation Deck, Photoshoot Balcony, Yongchun Pavilion

菲律賓榕 King's Fig、竹芋 Maranta、香楠 Incense Machilus、紅楠 Red Machilus、大葉楠 Large-leaved Machilus、黛粉葉 Dieffenbachia/Dumbcane;

雀榕 Decidous Fig、台灣山桂花 Taiwan Maesa、含笑 Port Wine Magnolia、竹柏 Asian Bayberry、五節芒 Silver-grass、風藤 Kadsura Pepper、杜英 Woodland Elaeocarpus;

珊瑚珠 Pigeonberry/Rougeplant、茄苳 Javanese Bishopwood、鵝掌柴/鴨腳木 Common Schefflera

🌿 回程沿途植物 Return Trip

水同木 (*Ficus fistulosa*) Common Yellow Stem-Fig、稜果榕 (*Ficus septica*) White-veined Fig/Septic Fig、鵝掌柴 / 鴨腳木 Common Schefflera、水冬瓜 (*Benincasa hispida*) Wax Gourd/White Gourd、觀音座蓮 (*Lotus nelumbo*) Sacred Lotus/Indian Lotus、絡石 (*Trachelospermum jasminoides*) Star Jasmine/Confederate, Jasmine、冷清草 Elatostema。

冷清草的邵語為 sailu，為蕁麻科樓梯草屬的植物。生長於海拔 200 米至 2,000 米的地區，多生長在山谷溝邊石上及林中灌叢中。

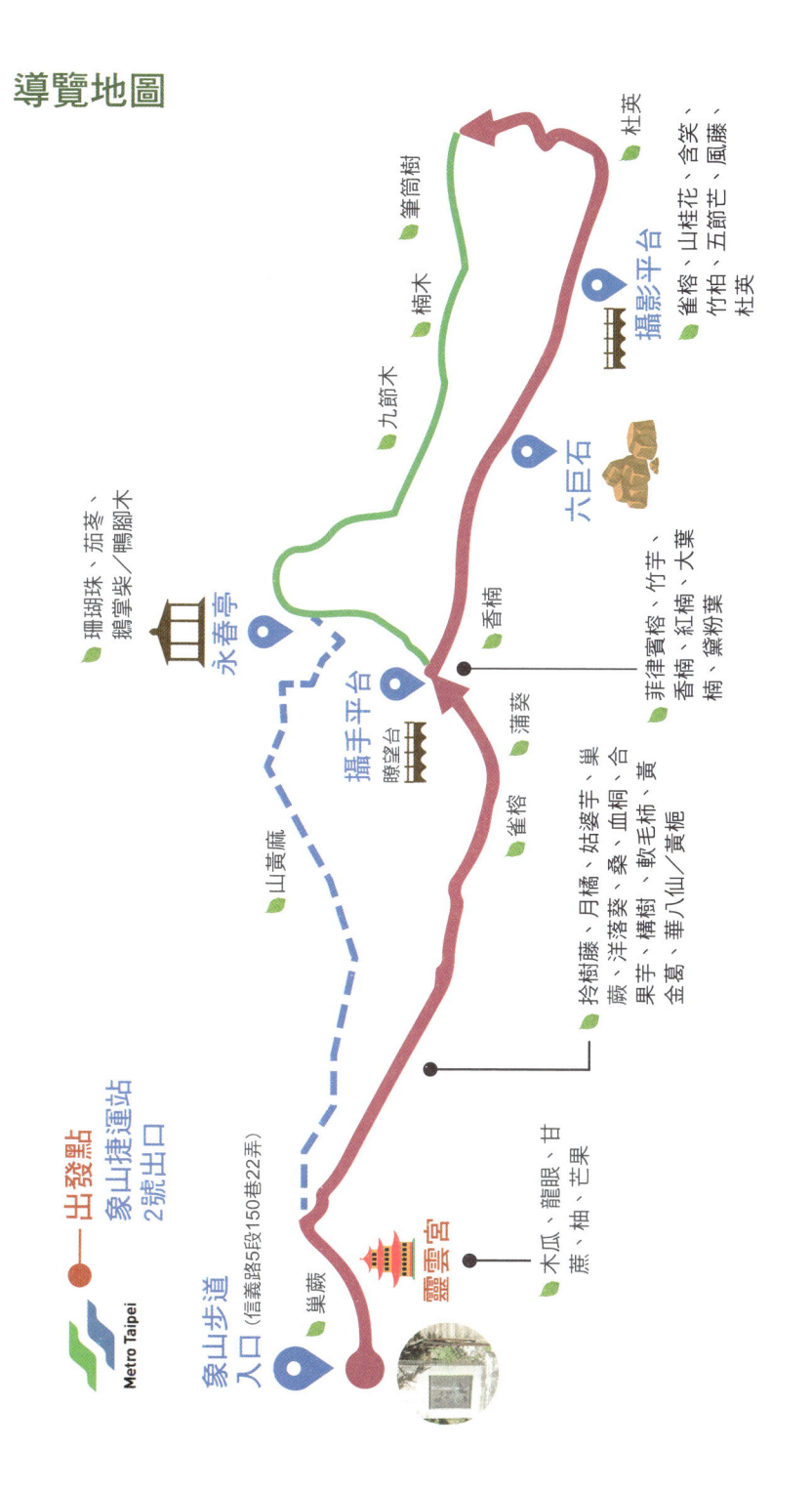

導覽地圖

出發點
象山捷運站
2號出口

象山步道
入口 (信義路5段150巷22弄)

Metro Taipei

巢蕨

靈雲宮

永春亭

珊瑚珠、茄苳、鵝掌柴／鴨腳木

筆筒樹

楠木

九節木

香楠

蒲葵

雀榕

山黃麻

攝手平台
瞭望台

六巨石

攝影平台

杜英

雀榕、山桂花、含笑、竹柏、五節芒、杜英

菲律賓榕、竹芋、紅楠、大葉香楠、黛粉葉

拎樹藤、月橘、姑婆芋、巢蕨、洋落葵、桑、血桐、果芋、構樹、軟毛柿、黃梔、金葛、華八仙／黃梔

木瓜、龍眼、甘蔗、柚、芒果

路線8　虎山

走過山澗步道，多識草木鳥獸之名
Hushan Hiking Trail: Plants in Literature

On the northwest side of the Nangang Mountain Range, you'll find the Four Beasts Mountains: Elephant Mountain, Lion Mountain, Leopard Mountain, and Tiger Mountain. Together, they make up the famous Four Beasts Mountain area.

Tiger Mountain is 140 meters high, sloping from west to east with wide, open views. The trail has a number of rest stops along the way, making it perfect for taking in the Taipei cityscape. Known for its rich biodiversity, the trail is a favorite among hikers and nature lovers, with a variety of plants and birds to discover. It's a great spot for a half-day eco-exploration.

How to Get There

Take bus 88 or Blue 10 to Fude Elementary School from MRT Xiangshan Station (Exit 2). From there, walk about 6–10 minutes along Lane 251 of Fude Street to reach the trailhead near Ci Hui Tang Temple. There is a huge sign that says "Four Beasts City Forest." The path to the left is the Tiger Mountain Natural Trail, and the one on the right is the Tiger Mountain Creek Trail.

What to Expect

The Creek Trail is a refreshing escape, with the gentle sound of running water and the chirping of birds and insects creating a peaceful atmosphere. The lush greenery makes it feel like you're stepping into another world. Along the creek, you'll find plenty of ferns, and if you look closely, you might spot fish, shrimp, frogs, or even fireflies in the valley.

The higher you go, the more the views open up. Before long, you'll have a perfect view of Taipei 101 rising proudly above the city.

Points of Interest

Tiger Mountain Creek, Vegetable Plot, Four Beasts Pavilion, Hushan Hiking Trails, Zhen Guang Zen Temple

English Introduction by: 林婉菁、林品妤、陳瑟娟、吳佳謙

台北南港山系的西北側，有「象山」、「獅山」、「豹山」及「虎山」四座山，統稱四獸山。

虎山是海拔 140 公尺的單面山，西高東低、視野遼闊，沿途皆有休憩平台，可眺望台北市景。虎山步道為台北市熱門健行路線，自然生態豐富，植物、鳥類種類眾多，適合做半日的生態觀察旅行。

虎山步道交通便利，由捷運象山站 2 號出口搭公車 88、藍 10 至福德國小站下，沿福德街 251 巷走約 6-10 分鐘，即可抵達慈惠堂登山口。福德街 251 巷底，有一「四獸山市民森林」巨碑，左手邊的山徑是虎山自然步道，右手邊是虎山溪山步道。

沿著虎山溪，潺潺水聲伴隨鳥叫蟲鳴，山澗步道綠意盎然，漫步其中彷彿身處世外。虎山溪沿岸有豐富的蕨類，溪谷中則孕育有魚、蝦、蛙類及螢火蟲等。循著虎山溪越往上走，視野就越遼闊，能清楚看到台北 101 大樓矗立。

虎山溪

The Hushan Hiking Trail (虎山自然步道) offers an enchanting retreat from the hustle and bustle of Taipei, winding through a lush, tranquil forest and alongside the gentle, murmuring waters of Hushan River. As you meander along the trail, the gently flowing waters of the Hushan River guide your way, providing a soothing soundtrack to your hike. Surrounded by a remarkable variety of flora, each species contributes its own unique charm to the landscape. Among the treasures, you will discover mulberry (桑); Japanese Cayratia Herb (五爪龍), a delicate vine with signature five-pronged leaves that grows prolifically along side rivers. The sweet fragrance of Common Jasmine Orange (月橘) mingles with the sharp scent of Fish Mint (魚腥草), guiding you along the way. You may catch sight of the grand Giant Elephant's Ear (姑婆芋), its oversized leaves casting cool shadows, offering shelter to smaller creatures. Along the way, the Taiwan Adina (水冬瓜) stands out as one of the most captivating plants. With its large, glossy leaves, it thrives in the damp, shaded areas along Hushan Creek. Encountering diverse plant life that showcases the richness of Taiwan's natural heritage, makes every step on the meandering path beside the Hushan River a discovery!

🌿 虎山溪沿途植物

桑 Mulberry、構樹 Paper Mulberry、五爪龍 / 烏蘞莓 Japanese Cayratia Herb、串鼻龍 Gourian Clematis、海金沙 Japanese Climbing Fern、三角葉西番蓮 Corkystem Passionflower、珊瑚珠 Pigeonberry/Rougeplant、龍眼 Longan、甘蔗 Sugarcane、月橘 Common Jasmine Orange、魚腥草 Fish Mint、姑婆芋 Giant Elephant's Ear、巢蕨 Bird's Nest Fern、黃金葛 Golden Pothos、血桐 Blush Macaranga/David's Heart、穿鞘花 Flower on Sheath、水同木 (*Ficus fistulosa*) Common Yellow Stem-Fig、稜果榕 (*Ficus septica*) White-veined Fig/Septic Fig、小毛蕨 Acuminate Cyclosorus、合果芋 Arrowhead Plant/Arrowhead Vine、鵝掌柴 Common Schefflera、黛粉葉 Dieffenbachia/Dumbcane、水冬瓜 Sinoadina/Taiwan Adina、觀音座蓮 Turnip Fern、冷清草 Elatostema、風藤 Kadsura Pepper、瑪瑙珠 Twoleaf Nightshade、紅樓花 Firespike/Cardinal Guard、山棕 Taiwan Sugar Palm、蛇莓 Mock Strawberry/Indian-strawberry、紫花酢醬草 Pink Woodsorrel、野桐 Japanese Mallotus/East Asian Mallotus、卷柏 Spike Moss、伏石蕨 Little-leaf Lemmaphyllum、菲律賓榕 King's Fig、野薑花 Butterfly Ginger Lily、菁芳草 Heartleaf Drymary、白匏子 Turn-in-the-wind

👣 菜園及四獸亭 (Vegetable Plot & Four Beasts Pavilion)

As you continue along the trail, you'll arrive at a vegetable plot created and maintained by the local community. Here, an enchanting mix of plants creates a tapestry of colors and textures. The heart-shaped leaves of the Madeira Vine（洋落葵）drapes gracefully along the path, while Shell Ginger（月桃）with its delicate blossoms adds a touch of elegance. Nearby, the glossy foliage of Mori Cleyera (森氏紅淡比) stands in harmony with the familiar Star Fruit (楊桃), whose unique star-shaped fruit might catch your eye. The resilient Chinaberry (苦楝) tree adds another layer of charm with its feathery branches swaying in the breeze.

Further along, the trail leads to the Four Beasts Pavilion (四獸亭), a peaceful spot to take in the surrounding beauty. Around this area, you'll find the broad leaves of Papaya (木瓜) trees, the deep-hued wood of Javanese Bishopwood (茄苳), and the cheerful, colorful clusters of *Lantana camara* (馬纓丹), which brighten the landscape with their vivid hues.

Every step through these diverse plant communities enriches your journey, adding vibrant life to the quiet allure of the trail.

菜園及四獸亭的植物

洋落葵 (*Anredera cordifolia*) Madeira Vine、月桃 Shell Ginger、森氏紅淡比 Mori Cleyera、楊桃 Carambola/Star Fruit、苦楝 Chinaberry、木瓜 Papaya、茄苳 Javanese Bishopwood、馬纓丹 (*Lantana camara*) Lantana

虎山自然步道 (Hushan Hiking Trail)

Walking along the trail, you'll find wild Melastoma scattered along the roadside, while the trail is surrounded by Formosa acacia and Red Machilus. Along the way, you'll also see Spanish Needles, Purple Woodnettles and Woodsorrels. Occasionally, the gentle fragrances of different fruit (Pomelo, Mango, Woolly-flowered Persimmon, and Canna) wafts through the air. If you visit in autumn or winter, the sight of Silver-grass adds a distinct winter atmosphere. The Hushan Hiking Trail is located in the Xinyi District of Taipei City and is easily accessible by public transportation. Entering from the bottom of Fude Street, Alley 251, you'll first see the "Si-Shou Shan Public Forest" stone tablet. To the left of the tablet is the Hushan Hiking Trail, and to the right is the Hushan River Mountain Trail.

🍃 虎山自然步道沿途植物

野牡丹 Melastoma、相思樹 (*Acacia confusa*) Formosa acacia、大花咸豐草 Beggarticks/Spanish Needles、紫麻 Purple Woodnettle、美人蕉 Canna、五節芒 Silver-grass、柚 Pomelo、芒果 Mango、島榕 Twiggy Fig、酢醬草（黃花）Woodsorrel、紅楠 Red Machilus、軟毛柿 Woolly-flowered Persimmon

👣 真光禪寺 (Zheng Guan Buddhist Temple)

Whichever trail you choose, after walking about fifteen minutes, you will arrive at Zheng Guan Buddhist Temple（真光禪寺）, a serene and spiritual sanctuary where you can pause, take your time, and make use of the restrooms. Nestled on the picturesque hillside, this tranquil religious center is surrounded by an abundance of lush greenery. The area is adorned with various plants, including the commonly seen Breadfruit trees（麵包樹）, the Large-leaf Deciduous Fig（大葉雀榕）, and the Chinese Hydrangea（華八仙）. These and other native flora come together to create a rich tapestry of natural beauty that perfectly complements the temple's serenity. The short walk to the temple offers a chance to leave behind the busy city and recharge in a peaceful, refreshing environment.

🌿 真光禪寺沿途植物

麵包樹 Breadfruit、冇骨消 Taiwan Elderberry、水金京 Formosan Wendlandia、華八仙 Chinese Hydrangea、大葉雀榕 Large-leaf Decidous Fig、台灣山桂花 Taiwan Maesa、破布子 Cordia/Fragrant Manjack、水芹 water celery、青剛櫟 Ringcupped Oak、紅楠 Machilus Thunbergii、刺杜密 Prickly Bridelia、三葉茀蕨 Selliguea hastata、筆筒樹 Brush Pot Tree Fern、台灣桫欏 Flying Spider-monkey Tree Fern、鬼桫欏 Black Tree Fern

▲ 野牡丹（引自 陳文彬《新細說台灣原生植物》）

▲ 台灣山桂花（引自 陳文彬《新細說台灣原生植物》）

▲ 鬼桫欏（引自 陳文彬《新細說台灣原生植物》）

導覽地圖

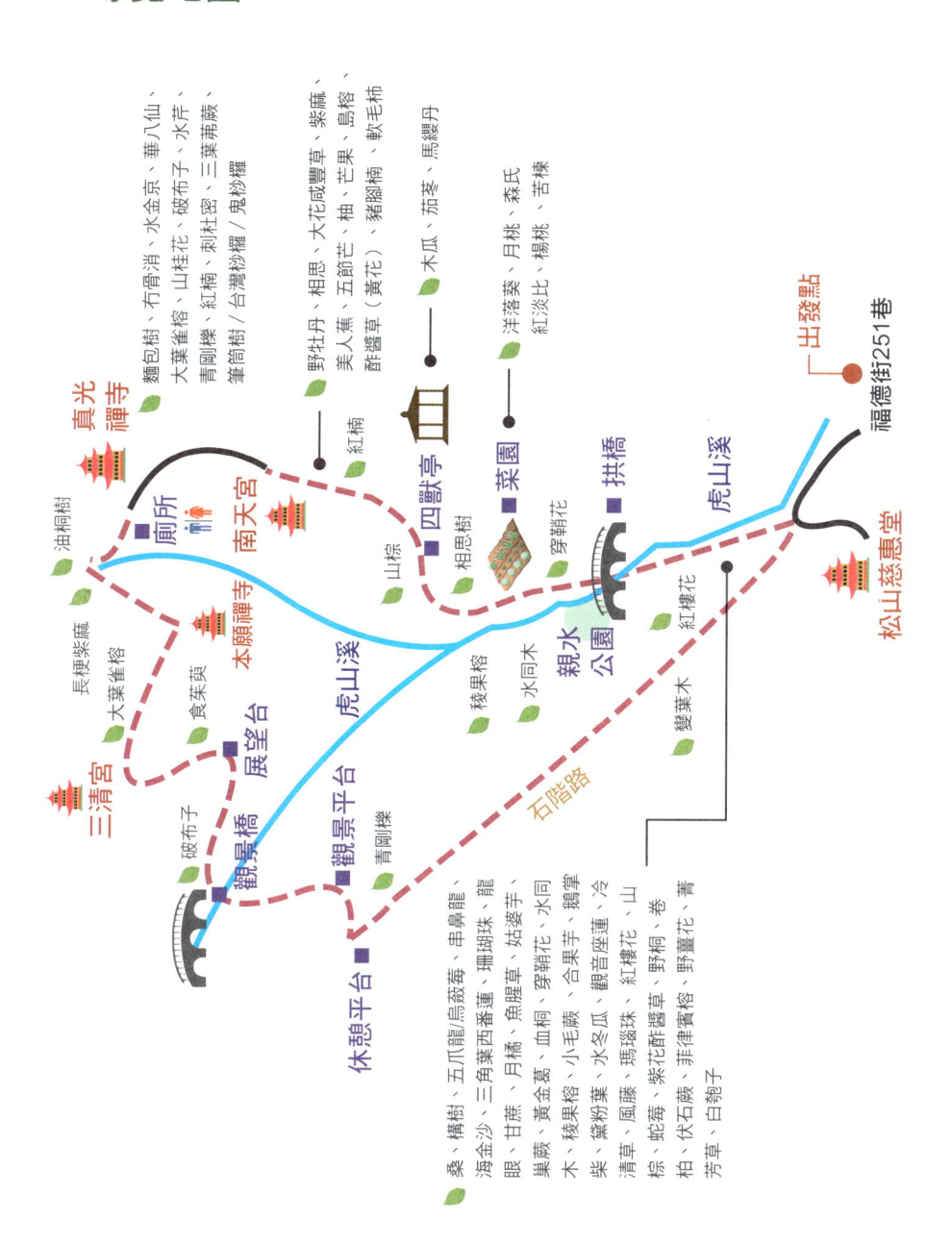

出發點：福德街251巷

松山慈惠堂

路線經過地點：
- 虎山溪
- 拱橋
- 菜園
- 四獸亭
- 南天宮
- 廁所
- 真光禪寺
- 油桐樹
- 本願禪寺
- 三清宮
- 展望台
- 觀景平台
- 景觀橋
- 休憩平台
- 親水公園
- 石階路

植物標示：

麵包樹、冇骨消、水金京、華八仙、大葉雀榕、山桂花、破布子、水芹、青剛櫟、紅楠、刺杜密、三葉崖爬藤、筆筒樹、台灣砂欏/鬼毛蕨

野牡丹、相思、大花咸豐草、紫薇、美人蕉、五節芒、柚、芒果、島榕、酢醬草（黃花）、豬腳楠、軟毛柿、馬纓丹

木瓜、茄苳、洋落葵、月桃、森氏紅淡比、楊桃、苦楝

長梗紫麻、大葉雀榕、食茱萸、山棕、相思樹、穗果榕、水同木、稜果榕、紅樓花、變葉木、破布子、青剛櫟

桑、構樹、五爪龍、三角葉西番蓮、珊瑚珠、串鼻龍、海金沙、甘蔗、月橘、魚腥草、姑婆芋、龍眼、黃金葛、黃荊、穿鞘花、水同木、巢蕨、稜果榕、小毛氈、合果芋、雞掌木、黛粉葉、水冬瓜、觀音座蓮、冷清草、風藤、瑪瑙珠、紅樓花、山棕、蛇莓、紫花酢醬草、野棉花、卷柏、伏石蕨、菲律賓榕、野薑花、菁芳草、白匏子

路線9 軍艦岩

發現植物人文與地質的美
Discover Beitou's Battleship Rock: A Hike Amongst Nature's Marvels

Battleship Rock (Junjianyan in Mandarin) perches atop hills north of the Taipei Veterans General Hospital and National Yang Ming Chiao Tung University's (NYCU) Yang Ming Branch, marking the southernmost peak of the Datun Mountain Range at an elevation of around 185 meters. The peak is entirely of sandstone, cemented from sand deposited undersea over 20 million years ago, then lifted above the ocean through tectonic activity. The trail stretches for about 3 km and offers hikers breathtaking views of unique natural rock formations. Situated along the northeasterly monsoon corridor, the ridgeline features a climate cooler than other places of similar elevation, allowing a variety of mid-to-high altitude and drought-tolerant plants, such as the hopbush, to flourish.

Transportation

1. Take the MRT to Shihpai MRT Station and exit through Exit 1, and then walk straight along Donghua Street Sec. 2 for 500 meters.
2. Turn right onto Linong Street Sec. 2 and walk into NYCU. The trailhead is inside the campus.

English Introduction by: 嚴浩文、彭國欣、劉驊、賴彥瑜

軍艦岩位於石牌榮總 / 陽明大學北方山區，是大屯山系最南端的一個山嶺，海拔約 185 公尺。軍艦岩的地質是兩千多萬年前海砂長期沈積之後膠結形成的砂岩，經由造山運動才隆起。登山步道約 3 公里，沿途可以欣賞特殊的自然地質景觀，因地處東北季風入口，氣溫較低，山脊線上可見一些原本生長在中高海拔的植物，以及耐乾旱的植物，如車桑子 (Hopbush) 等。捷運石牌站 1 號出口，沿東華街二段直行 500 公尺，右轉立農街二段抵陽明交通大學。

▲ 陽明大學正門口

🌿 陽明大學 U-bike 租借站附近植物

紫花酢漿草 Pink Woodsorrel、（黃花）酢漿草 Creeping Woodsorrel、蛇莓 Mock Strawberry、車前草 Plantain、金腰箭舅 Straggler Daisy、黃鵪菜 Japanese Youngia/Oriental False Hawksweed、南美蟛蜞菊 Bay biscayne creeping oxeye、大花咸豐草 Spanish Needles、構樹 Paper Mulberry、野桐 Japanese Mallotus、小葉欖仁 Madagascar Aalmond、山櫻花 Taiwan Cherry/Formosan Cherry、海桐 Pittosporum/Sticky Seed Tree、桑 Mulberry、姑婆芋 Giant Elephant's Ear、芒草 Silver Grass

▲ 紫花酢漿草 　　　▲ 山櫻花 　　　▲ 構樹

🌱 軍艦岩步道沿途植物

茄苳 Javanese Bishopwood、阿勃勒 Golden Shower Tree、月桃 Shell Ginger、血桐 Blush Macaranga/David's Heart、牽牛花 Morning Glory、島榕 Twiggy Fig、馬纓丹 Lantana、龍眼 Longan、美人蕉 Canna、九芎 Taiwan Crepe Myrtle、紫薇 Crepe Myrtle、合果芋 Arrowhead Plant/Arrowhead Vine、苧麻 Ramie、山黃麻 Oriental Trema、馬拉巴栗 Malabar Chestnut、台灣欒樹 Taiwan Goldenrain Tree、山黃梔 Cape Jasmine、粉黃纓絨花 Yellow Thistle、芒萁骨 Old World Forked Fern、烏桕 Chinese Tallow Tree、薜荔 Climbing Fig、白匏子 Turn-in-the-Wind、鵝掌柴 / 鴨腳木（江某） Common Schefflera、燈稱花 / 梅葉冬青 Rough-leaved Holly、野牡丹 Common Melastoma、車桑子 Hopbush、相思樹 Formosa Acacia、大頭茶 Fried Egg Plant、山菅蘭 / 桔梗蘭 Swordleaf

▲ 軍艦岩頂端風景（張雅雯 攝）

▲ 茄苳 　　　▲ 車桑子 　　　▲ 山黃梔

Dianella、楓香 Formosan Sweet Gum、呂宋莢迷 Luzon Viburnum、菝契 Roundleaf Greenbrier、青剛櫟 Ring-cupped Oak、八芝蘭竹 Pachilan Bamboo、盤龍木 / 牛筋藤 Burny Vine、長穗木 Nettleleaf Velvetberry、雙面刺 Shiny-leaf Prickly-ash、琉球松 Okinawa Pine/Luchu Pine、樟樹 Camphor Tree、香楠 Incense Machilus、細梗絡石 Star Jasmine、臺灣赤楠 Taiwan Syzygium、楊梅 Chinese Bayberry、毛蓮菜 / 地膽草 Elephant's Foot、桃金孃 Rose Myrtle

其他步道中可能會見到的植物

毬蘭 Porcelain Flower / Wax Plant、錫蘭饅頭果 Hong Kong Glochidion / Ceylon Gochidion、羅氏鹽膚木 Nutgall Tree / Roxburgh Sumac、拎壁龍 Creeping Pychotria、烏毛蕨 Oriental Blechnum (*Blechnum orientale*)、書帶蕨 (*Haplopteris flexuosa*) Sinuous Shoestring Fern、刺葉桂櫻 Black Thorn、鼠刺 Formosan Sweet Spire、台灣馬醉木 Formosa Pieris / Taiwan Pieris、米飯花 Don Blue Berry、羊角藤 Common Indian Mulberry、牛皮消 Formosan Swallowwort、大青 May Flower Glorybower、白柏 Taiwan Tallow Tree / Taiwan Sapium、灰木 (*Symplocos formosana*) Formosan Sweet Leaf

▲ 台灣馬醉木（引自《新細說台灣原生植物》）　▲ 拎壁龍（引自《新細說台灣原生植物》）

導覽地圖

■ 軍艦岩

臺灣赤楠、楊梅、
毛蓮菜、桃金孃

雙面刺、琉球松、樟樹、
香楠、細梗絡石

呂宋莢迷、菝契、青剛櫟、
八芝蘭竹、盤龍木、長穗木

馬拉巴栗、台灣欒樹、山黃梔、粉黃
纓絨花、芒萁骨、烏桕、薜荔、白匏
子、鵝掌柴/鴨腳木（江某）

茄苳、阿勃勒、月桃、血桐、牽牛花、
島榕、馬纓丹、龍眼、美人蕉、九芎、
紫薇、合果芋、苧麻、山黃麻

▲ 軍艦岩大學亭

燈稱花、野牡丹、車桑子、
相思樹、大頭茶、山菅蘭、楓香

▲ 唭哩岸山

軍艦岩親山步道
陽明交通大學登山口
出發點

陽明大學
ubike 租借站

紫花酢漿草、（黃花）酢漿
草、蛇莓、車前草、金腰箭、
莧、黃鵪菜、南美蟛蜞菊、
大花咸豐草、構樹、野桐、
小葉欖仁、山櫻花、海桐、
桑、姑婆芋、芒草

64

路線10 林語堂故居 / 尾崙古圳 / 狗殷勤古道
循先人足跡探訪文學中的植物
The Lin Yutang House, Gouyinqin Ancient Trail & Plants in Literature

The Lin Yutang House (林語堂故居) is nestled in the scenic hills of Yangmingshan in Taipei. You can take the Red 5 Bus from the MRT Shihlin Station to get there. After a twenty-minute ride, get off at Yongfu. Here, you'll be greeted by a tranquil haven that beautifully blends traditional Chinese aesthetics with touches of Western comfort. Along Yangde Boulevard, you'll be surrounded by lush greenery—Paper Mulberry with heart-shaped leaves, Golden Dewdrop with its clusters of bright golden berries, and Blush Macaranga that produces yellow-green flowers when in bloom, just to name a few. Let's keep going!

指福宮 Zifu Temple

Turn right at 168 Yangde Boulevard Section 2 and the Yangming Home for the Disabled bus stop. Follow Zhuangding Road, and you will see the small Zifu Temple, where locals worship Fuyou Dijun (Lü Dongbin, one of the Eight Immortals, who students and scholars revere as a deity). The temple is surrounded by a tranquil neighborhood. Along the way, you can observe the lush secondary forest on your left and the valley stream, with more trees, on your right. Here you can see plantains, which are mentioned in traditional Chinese poetry and also feature in the opening scene of Shakespeare's *Romeo and Juliet*.

Among other trees, there are "Turn-in-the-Wind" trees, whose leaves turn white in the fall, and Formosa Acacia, which is used as firewood. Additionally, finding out what locals plant here is quite worth noting. You can find papaya trees in their vegetable gardens!

柏園山莊 Boyuan Villa

As you stroll along the verdant paths, Boyuan Villa emerges gracefully, cradled by the lush landscapes on Yangmingshan. Built in the 1970s, this secluded retreat blends timeless elegance with natural splendor. The area is alive with vibrant colors of the Canna lilies lining the roads, while Giant Elephant's Ear and fragrant Shell Ginger create a tropical atmosphere. Majestic Banyan Trees provide cool, shaded trails, and clusters of delicate Lantana flowers attract fluttering butterflies. Boyuan Villa is where luxury meets the serene beauty of the mountains, offering a perfect sanctuary for nature lovers.

狗殷勤古道 Gouyinqin Ancient Trail

After passing the guard post at Boyuan Villa, walk more than ten meters to reach a fork in the path. To the left are three large Chinese Banyan trees with a viewing platform, where *Tetrastigma bioritsense* grow; to the right is a sign for "Weilun Ancient Canal, Pingdeng Village." Continuing along the concrete path, you'll find the Weilun Ancient Canal appears on your left. This path is known as the "Gouyinqin Ancient Trail." The roadside is lined with clusters of red-flowering canna. As you walk along the waterway, you'll also see many tree ferns, which have existed for about 250 million years, making them living fossils. The canal path is very gentle and easy to walk, while the continuous sound of flowing water provides a refreshing sense of tranquility.

English Introduction by: 林婉菁、林品妤、陳瑟娟、吳佳謙

陽明山坪頂地區的尾崙古圳路，由平等里的狗殷勤地區，通往公館里，是昔日農民通往山下的主要道路，又叫「狗殷勤古道」。狗慇勤即台語 kau-un-khun（狗塭睏），意味山上治安好，「狗」沒事「窩著睡」。從尾崙水圳路的入口至公平橋的菁礐（ㄑㄩㄝˋ）溪取水口，跨越公館里及平等里，路程約一個多小時，沿途水聲潺潺，綠蔭夾道，鳥語啁啾，蟲鳴蛙叫，是一條極佳的踏青路線。

從林語堂故居過馬路左轉，沿著仰德大道前行，途經永福里里民中心，沿途可見土地自己長出來的構樹、血桐、桑樹、虎葛（五爪龍）、月桃等原生植物及烏桕、大花咸豐草等歸化植物，也可看到人為植栽─南美朱槿、馬拉巴栗、金露花、炮仗花、阿勃勒等。

金露花原本叫台灣連翹，即吳濁流的作品《台灣連翹》中象徵台灣人命運的植物。1960 年代後園藝商人把「台灣連翹」改稱「金露華/金露花」，一方面是英文 Golden Dewdrop 的直譯，不過主要是搭當時火紅的美國影星金露華 (Kim Novak) 便車，金露華主演過《野宴》(*Picnic*, 1955) 及希區考克執導的《迷魂記》(*Vertigo*, 1958)。

在仰德大道二段 168 號，陽明教養院公車站牌右轉莊頂路前行，經指福宮，道路左邊山坡是竹林及次生林 (secondary forest/second-growth forest)，右下方是草木蔥蘢，綠意盎然的溪谷。

一路上可見詩經中歌詠的車前草，「采采芣苢，薄言采之。」

芣苢（ㄈㄨˊ一ˇ）即車前草，它也在莎士比亞的 *Romeo & Juliet* 第一幕中出現，叫 plantain；也可見到蜜源植物蒴藋（ㄕㄨㄛˋㄉㄧㄠˋ），又叫有骨消。此外還有秋風起時，滿山樹葉翻白的白匏子，鳥雀愛吃的雀榕，葉子形狀像台灣島的島榕，從前用來做薪柴、木炭的相思樹，以及孟子講的「三年之病，求七年之艾」的艾草，以及龍眼、朴樹、山黃麻、黃金葛、洋落葵（俗稱川七）、茄苳（重陽木）、青苧麻、羊蹄、金腰箭舅、葛藤等。途中也經過果菜園，種有木瓜等常見民生蔬果。

其中木瓜值得一提，詩經中「投我以木瓜，報之以瓊琚」的木瓜，指的是薔薇科 Chinese Quince 的果實。我們現在所說的木瓜 Papaya，正式名稱為番木瓜，是中南美洲引進的，現在則簡稱木瓜。

經過指福宮不久，可見一面開紫花的蔓馬纓丹構成的綠牆，柏園山莊四個大字赫然在目。

過柏園山莊警衛崗哨，旁邊有幾棵氣根懸垂的老榕樹。前行十餘公尺，叉路口左邊有三棵大榕樹，搭有觀景台，樹下有苗栗崖爬藤，右邊有「尾崙古圳、平等里」指示牌。從水泥小路上行，左側即尾崙古圳。路旁開紅花的美人蕉長成小聚落，也有成排的姑婆芋及月桃。美人蕉的花管有豐富的蜜汁，是從前小孩免費的甜點。姑婆芋又大又綠的葉子是魚販、肉販、果販愛用的綠襯，既可保濕，又可保鮮。月桃成串的花很漂亮，葉子可用來包糕粿，種子是提神藥品仁丹、口味兒的原料。

水泥小路的盡頭接馬路，是永公路 40 巷，與水圳平行，前行不久，馬路就與水圳分道揚鑣。沿水圳路直行，漸行漸窄，成為只能供人行的水圳路了。水圳沿山壁開鑿，一路水聲相伴，左有水圳水聲淙淙，右邊山谷亦不時傳來菁磐溪潺潺水聲。鳥語蟲鳴，松鼠跳躍樹間，饒富野趣。沿途植物種類繁多，有農家種植的波

蘿蜜、蓮霧、扶桑(朱槿)、咖啡樹，逸出或歸化的合果芋、王爺葵、蓖麻、象草，荒廢農園長出的芒草，著生在老樹上的崖薑蕨、伏石蕨、巢蕨(山蘇)，沿樹攀緣的風藤、拎樹藤，樹幹光溜溜的九芎，潮濕地區的冷清草、鴨跖草、三白草、山芹、毛茛、長梗苧麻、密花苧麻、水冬瓜、水同木，一般田園周遭常見的通泉草、山萵苣、苦苣菜、鵝兒腸、火炭母草、昭和草、山芥菜、薺菜、碎米薺，這裡也有，低海拔樹種紅楠、大葉楠、鵝掌柴(鴨腳木)更是到處可見。至於平地難以見到的楦(ㄑㄧ)葉懸鉤子、軟毛柿、雙面刺、觀音座蓮、山棕、山桂花等，這裡則不難看到。

　　途中也可見到不少筆筒樹，筆筒樹自距今 2.5 億年三疊紀時代即存在於地球，是名符其實的活化石。

　　抵公平橋之前不遠，路旁有一小小的古老石棚土地公，百年來默默保佑行走古道上民眾一路平安。公平橋建於 1987 年，跨越菁礐溪，橋下有尾崙水圳取水口。過橋左邊有座木造涼亭，旁有小路可下到溪畔戲水。直行沿花崗石階路向上，則脫離水圳，通往平等里 42 巷的狗殷勤地區，一路得爬升 100 公尺，約 20 分鐘。

🍃 林語堂故居周遭植物（士林區仰德大道二段 141 號）

構樹 Paper Mulberry、血桐 Blush Macaranga/David's Heart、桑樹 Mulberry、虎葛(五爪龍) Japanese Cayratia Herb、月桃 Shell Ginger、烏桕 Chinese Tallow-tree、大花咸豐草 Beggarticks/Spanish Needles、（人為植栽）南美朱槿 Chinese Hibiscus、馬拉巴栗 (*Pachira macrocarpa*) Malabar Chestnut、金露花 (金露華 / 台灣連翹) (*Duranta erecta*) Golden Dewdrop、炮仗花 Flame Vine、阿勃勒 (*Cassia fistula*) Golden Shower Tree

🍃 指福宮周遭植物（士林區莊頂路 141 號）

車前草 (苤苢) Plantain、密源植物：蕗蕎 (有骨消) Taiwan Elderberry、白匏子 Turn-in-the-Wind、雀榕 Decidous Fig、島榕 Twiggy Fig、相思樹 (*Acacia confusa*) Formosa Acacia、艾草 Silvery Wormwood/Chinese Mugwort、龍眼 Longan、朴樹 Chinese Hackberry、山黃麻 Oriental Trema、黃金葛 Golden Pothos、洋落葵 (川七) (*Anredera cordifolia*) Madeira Vine、茄苳 (重陽木) Javanese Bishopwood、青苧麻 (*Boehmeria nivea*) False Nettle、羊蹄 Bauhinia、金腰箭舅 Straggler Daisy、葛藤 Kudzu、蔓馬纓丹 Trailing Lantana

🍃 柏園山莊周遭植物（士林區莊頂路 168 號）

榕樹 Chinese Banyan、苗栗崖爬藤 *Tetrastigma bioritsense*、美人蕉 Canna Lily、姑婆芋 Giant Elephant's Ear、月桃 Shell Ginger

🍃 尾崙古圳、狗殷勤古道周遭植物

波羅蜜 Jackfruit、蓮霧 Jambu、扶桑 (朱槿) Chinese hibiscus、咖啡樹 coffee、合果芋 Arrowhead Plant/Arrowhead Vine、王爺葵 Giant Mexican Sunflower、蓖麻 Castor Oil Plant、象草 Elephant Grass、芒草 Silvergrass、崖薑蕨 Basket Fern、伏石蕨 Little-leaf Lemmaphyllum、巢蕨 (山蘇) Bird's Nest Fern、風藤 Kadsura Pepper、拎樹藤 dragon-tail plant、九芎 Crepe Myrtle、冷清草 Elatostema、鴨跖草 Asiatic Dayflower、三白草 Asian Lizard's Tail、山芹 Ostericum、毛茛 Japanese Buttercup、長梗紫麻 Purple Woodnettle、密花苧麻 Dense-flowered False-nettle、水冬瓜 Sinoadina/Taiwan Adina、水同木 (*Ficus fistulosa*) Common Yellow Stem-Fig、通泉草 Japanese Mazus/Asian Mazus、山

萵苣 Wild Lettuce、苦苣菜 Field Sowthisle、鵝兒腸 Water Chickweed、火炭母草 Creeping Smartweed、昭和草 Redflower Ragleaf、山芥菜/葶菜 Yellowcress、薺菜 Shepherd's Purse、碎米薺 Hairy Bittercress、紅楠 Red Machilus、大葉楠 Large-leaved Machilus、鵝掌柴 (鴨腳木) Common Schefflera、榿葉懸鉤子 Alder-leaf Raspberry、軟毛柿 Woolly-flowered Persimmon、雙面刺 Shiny-leaf Prickly-ash、觀音座蓮 Turnip Fern、山棕 Taiwan Sugar Palm、台灣山桂花 Taiwan Maesa、筆筒樹 Brush Pot Tree Fern

▲ 車前草（蘇恆隆 攝）

▲ 大花咸豐草（蘇恆隆 攝）

導覽地圖

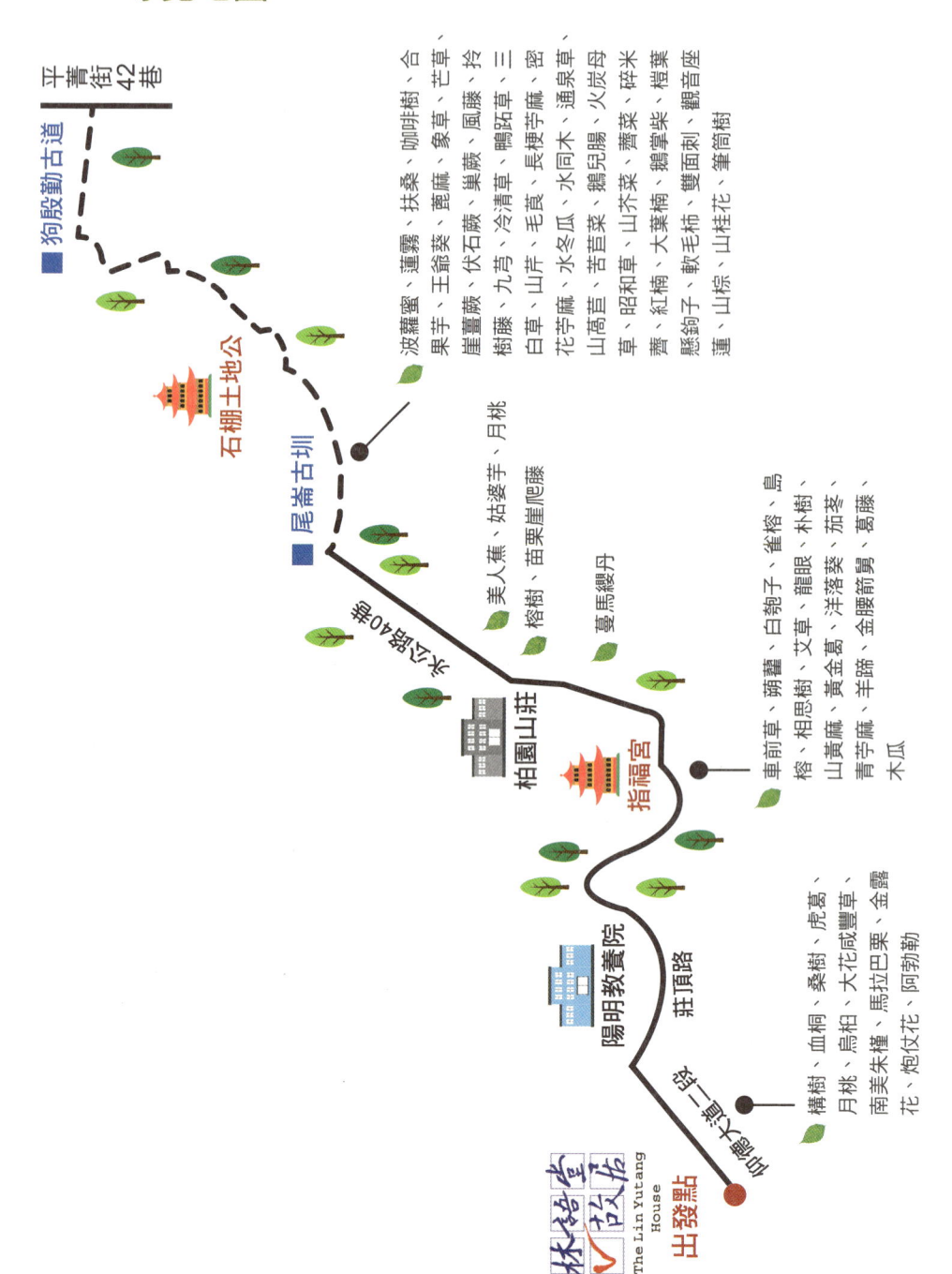

狗殷勤古道 — 平菁街42巷

波羅蜜、蓮霧、扶桑、咖啡樹、合果芋、王爺葵、鹿蕨、象草、芒草、崖薑蕨、伏石蕨、巢蕨、風藤、玲樹藤、九芎、冷清草、鴨跖草、三白草、山芹、毛柔、長梗苧蕨、密花菅蕨、水冬瓜、水同木、通泉草、山高苣、苦苣菜、鵝兒腸、火炭母草、昭和草、山芥菜、薺菜、碎米薺、紅楠、大葉楠、鵝掌柴、橙米懸鉤子、軟毛柿、雙面刺、觀音座蓮、山棕、山桂花、筆筒樹

石棚土地公

尾崙古圳

水公路400地

美人蕉、姑婆芋、月桃
榕樹、苗栗崖爬藤
蔓馬纓丹

柏園山莊

指福宮

車前草、葫蘆、白匏子、雀榕、島榕、相思樹、艾草、龍眼、朴樹、山黃麻、黃金葛、洋落葵、茄苳、青芋蕨、羊蹄、金腰前胡、葛藤、木瓜

陽明教養院

莊頂路

林語堂故居 The Lin Yutang House

出發點 — 仰德大道二段

構樹、血桐、桑樹、虎葛、月桃、相柏、大花咸豐草、南美朱槿、馬拉巴栗、金露花、炮仗花、阿勃勒

植物的葉子

陳文彬

植物的根吸收土壤裡的水分和礦物質；葉子裡由葉綠素利用光能，將水和二氧化碳合成醣類的特殊功能，稱為光合作用（photosynthesis）。所以葉子是植物的營養器官。綠色植物利用光能將無機物的水和二氧化碳合成有機物的醣類，我們稱之為自營生物（autotroph）。有些植物的植物體並無葉綠素，所以無法行光合作用，異營生物不能將無機物合成本身所需的養分，必須以自營生物或已腐敗的有機物維生。所有的動物、菌類以及大部分的細菌皆為異營生物（heterotroph）。

異營生物（heterotroph）者，若生活於其他動物或植物的體內或體表，自寄主（host）獲得養分者稱寄生物（parasite）。

有些植物既不能自行製造養分，也不能攝取固體食物，而只能吸收已經分解的養分，這種異營方法叫做腐生（saprotroph）。例如本書中敘述的水晶蘭。

辨識種子植物時，花是首要觀察的特徵，但在一年中大部分開花植物的花期是短暫的，所以葉子就成為在野外辨識種子植物時的重要標的。

茲將觀察葉子的重要特徵分述如下：

一、葉子的各部位名稱

以黃槿為例，如圖片所標示：

1. 葉柄（petiole）。
2. 葉尖或稱先端（apex）：銳尖（acute）。
3. 葉基（base）：心形（cordate）。
4. 葉脈（venation）。

以蘆葦為例，如圖片所標示：

5. 葉片（blade）。
6. 葉鞘（sheath）。
7. 葉舌（ligule）：單子葉植物的葉子在葉片和葉鞘連接處的內側有一膜質或纖毛狀的突起物稱為葉舌。
8. 葉耳（auricle）：葉片的基部兩側有時有一對耳狀突起物稱為葉耳，它也是葉基的一部分。
9. 托葉（stipule）：
    以墨點櫻桃為例的腋生托葉。
    以毛玉葉金花為例的側生托葉。
10. 葉緣（margin）：
    例如：墨點櫻桃的葉緣為全緣（entire）。
    而其腋生托葉的葉緣為鋸齒緣（serrulate）。
    第倫桃的葉緣為牙齒緣（dentate）。
    櫻花的葉緣為重鋸齒緣（doubly serrate）。

植物的葉子

▲ 黃槿
- 葉基 base — 心形 cordate
- 葉柄 petiole
- 葉脈 venation
- 葉尖 apex — 銳尖 acute

▲ 蘆葦
- 葉片 blade
- 葉舌 ligule
- 葉耳 auricle
- 葉鞘 sheath

▲ 墨點櫻桃
- 腋生托葉 axillary stipule
- 葉緣 margin
- 鋸齒緣 serrulate
- 全緣 entire
- 托葉 stipule

▲ 毛玉葉金花
- 側生托葉 lateral stipule
- 葉片 blade
- 托葉 stipule

▲ 第倫桃
- 牙齒緣 dentate

▲ 櫻花
- 重鋸齒緣 doubly serrate

75

二、葉序（phyllotaxis）

葉子在莖或枝上的排列方式。

1. 互生（alternate）：枝上的每一節上僅生有一片葉子，且依序一左一右互相排列。例如：白珠樹。
2. 對生（opposite）：枝上的每一節上生有兩片葉子。例如：向天盞（半枝蓮）。
3. 十字對生（decussate）：對生的一種，但上下兩對葉子方向交叉的角度近乎直角而成十字形。例如：台灣及己。
4. 輪生（whorled，verticillate）：莖、枝上的每一節上著生三片以上的葉子而成輪狀者。例如：黑板樹。
5. 叢生（fasciculate）：莖上節間短，且葉子密集著生三片以上者。例如：蒲葵。

三、葉脈

以菩提樹為例，如圖片標示：

1. **依粗細和分化：**
    A. 中肋（主脈）（midrib）。
    B. 側脈（lateral vein）。
    C. 網脈（reticulate vein）。
2. **依在葉片分佈與走向。**
    A. 掌狀脈（palmate venation），例如：山芙蓉。
    B. 平行脈（parallel venation），例如：船子草。
    C. 羽狀脈（pinnate venation），例如：第倫桃。
    D. 放射脈（radiating venation），例如：金蓮花。

植物的葉子

互生 alternate

對生 opposite

▲ 白珠樹

▲ 向天盞

十字對生 decussate

▲ 台灣及己

叢生 fasciculate

輪生 whorled, verticillate

莖 stem

葉 leaf

▲ 黑板樹

▲ 蒲葵

▲ 菩提樹

▲ 山芙蓉

▲ 船子草

羽狀脈
pinnate venation

放射脈
radiating venation

▲ 第倫桃　　▲ 金蓮花

四、單葉（simple leaf）與複葉（compound leaf）

1. **單葉（simple leaf）**：葉片單一，不分裂成許多小裂片。例如：烏臼。

2. **複葉（compound leaf）**：葉片分裂成許多小片，各小片稱為小葉（leaflet），小葉本身若有葉柄，就稱為小葉柄（petiolule）。

複葉又分：

A. **掌狀複葉（palmate compound leaf）**：小葉在總葉柄頂端著生，展開成掌狀。 例如：鵝掌藤。

B. **羽狀複葉（pinnate compound leaf）**：側生小葉排列在葉軸的兩側成羽毛狀的複葉。又可分：

(1) 奇數羽狀複葉（odd-pinnate compound leaf）：
　　(a) 奇數羽狀複葉──例如：台灣魚藤。
　　(b) 二回奇數羽狀複葉（odd-bipinnately compound leaf）──例如：台灣欒樹、三回至多回奇數羽狀複葉（multi-pinnate leaf），例如：南天竹。
(2) 偶數羽狀複葉（even-pinnate compound leaf）：
　　(a) 一回偶數羽狀複葉──例如：阿勃勒。
　　(b) 二回偶數羽狀複葉──例如：美洲合歡。
　　──餘類推。

C. 就小葉數目分：

(1) 單身複葉（simple compound leaf）──例如：柚葉藤，柚子。
(2) 三出複葉（ternate compound leaf）──例如：魚木。
──餘類推。

五、托葉（stipule）

並非所有植物的葉子都具有托葉，例如夾竹桃科植物則無托葉，茜草科植物則具有托葉。

1. **腋生托葉（axillary stipule）**：托葉著生於葉腋處。例如：墨點櫻桃。

2. **側生托葉（lateral stipule）**：托葉著生於葉柄兩側。例如：台灣鉤藤。

植物的葉子

單葉
simple leaf

▲ 烏桕

小葉
leaflet

小葉柄
petiolule

掌狀複葉
palmate compound leaf

葉柄
petiole

▲ 鵝掌藤

小葉柄
petiolule

奇數羽狀複葉
odd-pinnate compound leaf

▲ 台灣魚藤

二回奇數羽狀複葉
odd-bipinnately compound leaf

▲ 台灣欒樹

三回至多回奇數羽狀複葉
multi-pinnate leaf

▲ 南天竹

一回偶數羽狀複葉
even-pinnate compound leaf

▲ 阿勃勒

81

二回偶數羽狀複葉
even-bipinnate
compound leaf

▲ 美洲合歡

單身複葉
simple compound leaf

▲ 柚葉藤

三出複葉
ternate compound leaf

▲ 魚木

莖
stem

葉柄
petiole

葉片
blade

側生托葉
lateral stipule

▲ 台灣鉤藤

花事知多少？

陳文彬

一、甚麼是花？

被子植物（Angiosperm）的生殖器官稱為花（flower）。花由花萼（calyx）、花冠（corolla）、雄蕊（stamen）和雌蕊（pistil）4部分組成。

1. 花萼（calyx）

萼片（sepals）位於花的最外層，常為綠色的葉狀器官，萼片的全體合稱花萼。如果萼片彼此完全分離，則稱此花萼為離生萼

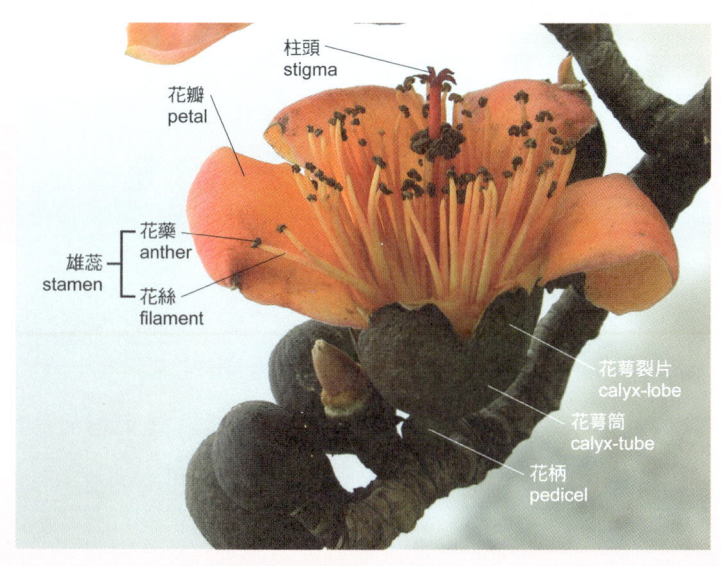

▲ 以木棉花的合生萼為例，標示雙子葉植物花各部位名稱。

（polysepalous calyx）。如果萼片或多或少是合生，則稱此花萼為合生萼（symsepalous calyx）。

合生萼連合的部分，一般稱為花萼筒（calyx-tube），分離部分稱為花萼裂片（calyx-lobe），有些植物花萼的外層有一輪苞片，稱為副萼（epicalyx）。

▲ 八角蓮的離生萼。 　　　　▲ 朱槿的合生萼與副萼。

2. 花冠（corolla）

花瓣（petals）是位於花萼內層的葉狀器官，通常色澤豔麗，會招蜂引蝶，花冠就由全體花瓣組成。如果各花瓣彼此完全分離，則稱此花冠為離瓣花冠（choripetalous corolla），這樣的花稱為離瓣花。

如果花瓣或多或少是合生，則稱此花冠為合瓣花冠（symsepalous corolla），這樣的花稱為合瓣花。

花冠合生部分，稱為花冠筒（corolla-tube），分離部分稱為花冠裂片（corolla-lobe）。少數種類花冠筒與花萼部份合生，例如：萎蕤。

3. 花被（perianth）

　　花的最外兩輪若由無法區分花萼和花冠組成，合稱花被，所以組成花被的萼裂片和花瓣統稱為花被片（tepal），常使用於樟科、百合科……等。

4. 雄蕊（stamen）

　　位於花冠的內層，由花絲（filament）和花藥（anther）組成。

5. 雌蕊（pistil）

　　位於花的中心，由子房（ovary）、花柱（style）和柱頭（stigma）組成。

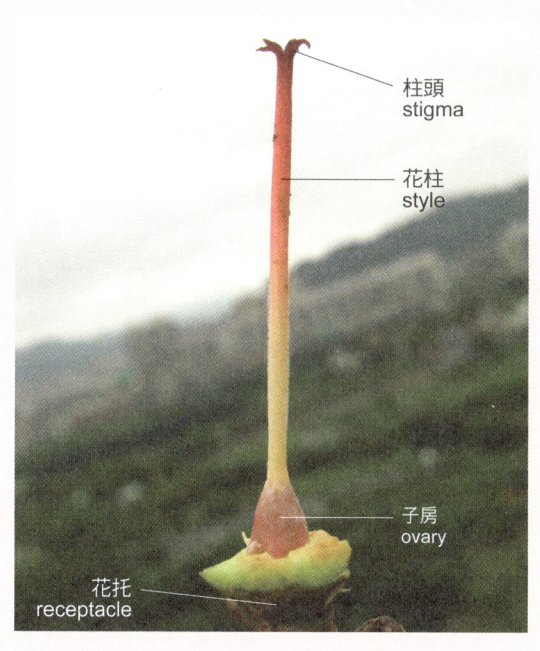

▲ 以木棉花為例標示雙子葉植物雌蕊各部位名稱。

▲ 以大青為例看合瓣花和合生萼。

二、花的性別

1. 單性花（unisexual）

　　僅具有雄蕊或雌蕊的花，稱之為單性花。一朵花如果僅具有雄蕊和不孕性的退化雌蕊，仍視為雄性的單性花；同樣，一朵花如果具有雌蕊和不孕性的退化雄蕊，仍視為雌性的單性花。如果單性花、雌花和雄花生於不同的植株上，稱為雌雄異株（dioecious）。如果單性花、雌花和雄花生於同一植株上，稱為雌雄同株（monoecious）。

2. 兩性花（bisexual）

　　一朵花如果同時存在雄蕊與雌蕊者，稱為兩性花。例如：山櫻花。

▲ 鐵冬青的單性花；雌花有退化雄蕊。

▲ 鐵冬青的單性花；雄花有退化雌蕊。

雄花 male flower
雌花 female flower

▲ 烏桕的單性花，無花被，雌雄同株。

3. 雜性花（polygamous）

兩性花與單性花同生在一植株上者，稱為雜性花。例如：中原氏鼠李。

三、完全花與不完全花

1. 完全花（complete flower）

一朵花如果具有花萼、花瓣、雄蕊和雌蕊 4 部分的，稱為完全花。

▲ 赤車使者，無花瓣，花被 5 裂，是為不完全花。

▲ 瓜子金的花形左右對稱，萼片 5 枚，花瓣 3 枚不等長，是為不整齊花。

2. 不完全花（incomplete flower）

一朵花如果缺少花萼、花瓣、雄蕊和雌蕊 4 者中任一部分，稱為不完全花。

四、整齊花與不整齊花

1. 整齊花（regular flower）

花萼與花瓣大小相等，形狀相同的花稱為整齊花。例如：山豬肝。

2. 不整齊花（irregular flower）

花萼裂片大小不相等、形狀不相同，花瓣大小不相等、形狀不相同的花稱為不整齊花。

五、雌蕊的離生心皮和合生心皮

1. 雌蕊（pistil）

完全的雌蕊是由子房（ovary）、花柱（style）和柱頭（stigma）3部份組成。

2. 心皮（carpel）

心皮是組成雌蕊的單位。

3. 離生心皮子房（apocarpous ovary）

雌蕊若是由彼此分離的心皮組成者，稱為離生心皮子房。例如：木蘭科、昆欄樹科、八角茴香科、五味子科和毛茛科等植物的雌蕊。

4. 合生心皮子房（syncarpous ovary）

雌蕊若是由2個以上的心皮彼此癒合組成者，稱為合生心皮子房。例如：牻牛兒苗科植物為5枚合生心皮子房。

▲ 昆欄樹的雌蕊是為離生心皮子房。

六、苞片（bract）與小苞片（bracteole，bractlet）

1. 苞片（bract）
生於花梗或花序下，或花序每一分枝基部的葉狀或鱗片狀器官稱為苞片。

2. 小苞片（bracteole）
生於花梗上或花萼下的葉狀或鱗片狀器官稱為小苞片。

▲ 以銹毛鐵線蓮為例，看苞片和小苞片。

七、花序（inflorescence）

花在花枝上排列的次序稱為花序。花如果有小柄，就稱為花柄（pedicel）。花柄著生在花軸（rachis），未著生花的花軸下部稱為花梗（peduncle）。

八、繖形花序（umbel）

1. 單一繖形花序（simple umbel）
花梗的頂端呈放射狀著生等長的花，成為平頂，稱為單一繖形花序。

▲ 以野當歸為例標示複繖形花序。

2. 複繖形花序（compound umbel）

花梗的頂端著生等長的花軸（rachis），而各花軸頂端為多數等長的花柄（pedicel），且著生放射狀平頂的花，稱為複繖形花序。

九、葇荑花序（catkin, ament）

屬穗狀、總狀、聚繖花序狀，但必須是單性花又無花瓣，花多而細小，無花柄或近無花柄，由小苞片或葉狀苞片襯托。例如：殼斗科、楊柳科植物……等。

十、單一聚繖花序（simple dichasium）

花枝的主軸頂端著生一朵花，其下方有兩分枝對生，枝頂也各生一朵花，稱為單一聚繖花序。

走讀自然・花言樹語

| 花藥 | 花絲 | 小苞片 | 腺體 |
| anther | filament | bractlet | gland |

▲ 水柳的雌性葇荑花序。

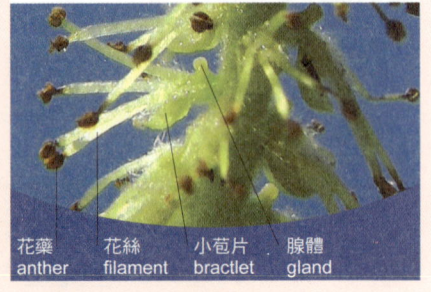

▲ 水柳的雄性葇荑花序。

▲ 銹毛鐵線蓮的單一聚繖花序。

花言樹語

談植物的學名及字源
Scientific Name & Etymology

世界各國的植物都有自己語言的名稱，美國的植物家會知道當地植物的學名及英文名稱，臺灣的植物學家通常也知道植物的學名及中文名稱。不過如果美國的植物學家告訴你，某種植物的中文名字叫什麼，或臺灣的植物學家告訴你，某一種植物的英文名稱叫什麼？你不可以完全相信，因為他們可能是間接得來的訊息，有可能弄錯。但他們之間有一個共同的基礎 (common denominator)，不會混淆，那就是學名 (scientific name)。學名是用拉丁語來表示，名稱統一，世界各國都能互通。

每種植物的學名由兩個部分構成：第一個字是屬名 (generic name)，字首必須大寫，斜體，第二個字是種小名 (specific epithet)，斜體，首字母不用大寫。

A scientific name consists of two words: the generic name and the specific epithet. The generic name is the genus to which the species belongs, and the specific epithet refers to the species within that genus. For example, in the name *Chionanthus retusus*, 'Chionanthus' is the genus name and 'retusus' is the specific epithet.

譬如台灣原生植物「流蘇」，英文叫 Chinese fringe tree，學名是 *Chionanthus retusus*，學名的第一個字 *Chionanthus* 就是屬名，字首須大寫，斜體；第二個字 *retusus* 是種小名，又稱種加詞，也是斜體，但首字母不用大寫。

▲ 流蘇 *Chionanthus retusus*（引自 陳文彬《新細說台灣原生植物》）

又如：「白花苜蓿」(白花三葉草)，學名是 *Trifolium repens* L.

Trifolium 是屬名 + *repens* 是種小名 + L. 是命名者林奈 Linnaeus 的縮寫，但不用斜體，要用正體。

這種命名規則叫 Binominal Nomenclature，二名法，又稱雙名法，是 1753 年 Carl Linnaeus 在他的曠世鉅作 *Species Plantarum* 中正式引介的物種命名系統。

植物學名是用拉丁文來表示植物特徵、原生地等，但字源有可能來自希臘文或其他語文的拉丁化。如近年來流行的「紅藜」，英文叫 red quinoa，學名是 *Chenopodium formosanum*，

Chenopodium 希臘文的意思是葉子形狀像鵝腳；*formosanum* 就是臺灣的形容詞，所以有人主張中文名應正名為「臺灣藜」。

Chenopodium formosanum is a *Chenopodium* species native to Taiwan. It was a key component of the diets of Taiwanese indigenous peoples and remains culturally and culinarily significant. *Chenopodium formosanum* is known in the Paiwan language as djulis. The generic name *Chenopodium* is derived from the particular shape of the leaf, which is similar to a goose's foot: from Greek χήν (chen), "goose" and πούς (pous), "foot" or ποδίον (podion), "little foot". (Chenopodium – Wikipedia)

要怎樣找出植物學名字源的意義？你只要把「白花苜蓿」學名後面加上 etymology 去 Google，譬如："Trifolium repens" etymology，就會出現：

The genus name, Trifolium, derives from the Latin tres, "three", and folium, "leaf", so called from the characteristic form of the leaf, which almost always has three leaflets (trifoliolate); hence the popular name "trefoil". The species name, repens, is Latin for "creeping". 因此我們知道 Trifolium 是「三葉」草，repens 就是「在地上爬」。

▲ 白花苜蓿 Trifolium repens （朱敏禎 攝）

同樣我們也可以知道,「流蘇」學名第一個字 *Chionanthus*,是「雪花」之意,chion 意即 snow,anthos 是 flower。(chion = snow; anthos = flower). Norton Anthology (諾頓文選) 的 Anthology,本義就是「名花薈萃」。

美人蕉 (*Canna indica*) 學名裡的 Canna 是 cane, reed like 之意,因美人蕉的莖細圓如手杖或蘆桿;而 indica 在這裏是指西印度群島,不是指印度。

譬如你查花椰菜的字源,就知道它的本意是「花長在莖上」。Cauliflower Etymology. New Latin; from caulis ("stem") + flōs ("flower") They are grown for their thickened, profuse, undeveloped flowers and flower stalks instead of for their leaves.

又如你查木棉樹 (*Bombax ceiba*),就知道它字源的本意是「果實裡有 silky hairs 的大樹」。The genus comes from the Greek bombyx meaning silk in reference to the silky hairs in the seed capsule. The epithet comes from a Spanish derivative name referring to a group of large, tropical trees related to Bombax. ceiba /ˈsʌɪbə/ via Spanish from Taino, literally 'giant tree'.

野牡丹 (*Melastoma candidum*) 的屬名 *Melastoma*,Mela,就是黑,stoma 是嘴巴;意思是吃了嘴巴會變黑。The genus *Melastoma* means 'black mouth' and refers to the seeds of some plants in the genus which can stain the mouth black.

類似的還有「白千層」,英文叫 weeping paperbark,學名叫 *Melaleuca*。Mela 就是黑,leuca 就是白的意思。The name *Melaleuca* is derived from the Ancient Greek μέλας (mélas) meaning "dark" or "black" and λευκός (leukós) meaning "white", apparently because one of the first specimens described had fire-blackened white bark. 「白千層」葉子含油量很高，容易引起森林大火，火災過後，樹皮有黑有白，因此叫 Melaleuca。

順便一提，近年來流行的所謂茶樹精油，其實是「細葉白千層」(Melaleuca alternifolia) 的葉子提煉的。Tea tree oil is distilled from the leaves of the Melaleuca alternifolia plant, found in Australia.

又，「掌葉蘋婆」學名 *Sterculia foetida* 的意思：第一個字是糞便之神 *Sturculius*，第二個字 foetida 是臭味，指它開花

▲ 細葉白千層 Melaleuca alternifolia（陳宗裕 攝）

的味道。Etymology: The genus "Sterculia" is named after the Roman god Sterculius, the god of manure. The reference is to the foul-smelling flowers of some species in this genus. The species epithet "foetida" means foul-smelling, referring to the flower's aroma.

「杜鵑花」在英美一般比較喜歡說 rhododendron，它的字源意思是，開像玫瑰一樣美麗花的樹。(Rhododendron, via Latin from Greek, from rhodon 'rose' + dendron 'tree') 臺灣學校裡教「杜鵑花」的英文卻是 azalea。

以下是綜合美國園藝專家對 azalea 與 rhododendron 兩者的區別的看法：

All azaleas are rhododendrons but not all rhododendrons are azaleas. Most azaleas are deciduous, but true rhododendrons are usually evergreen. Azaleas are small to medium sized shrubs with many, smaller stems whilst rhododendrons tend to be larger plants with fewer stout stems.

也就是說 rhododendrons 可以涵蓋 azalea，但 azalea 不能涵蓋 rhododendron，因此 rhododendron 是比較保險的說法。

最後，我要談一下學名對於譯者及從事英文教育者的用處。如果我們碰到一些臺灣沒有的植物，還沒有中文名字，或者在英美還沒有英文名字的植物，或者現有英文譯名不理想的，我們可以根據植物拉丁學名的意義來譯成中文或英文。譬如「島榕」的學名是 *Ficus virgata*，拉丁文 Ficus = fig，virgata = twiggy。

臺灣最主要的植物網站 biodiv.tw http://kplant.biodiv.tw，把島榕的英文譯為 "Philippine Fig"、"White-flesh Fig"。Philippine Fig 會與真正的「菲律賓榕」(*Ficus ampelas*) 混淆，White-flesh Fig 大概是從俗名白肉榕直譯，兩個英文名字都不理想，可據拉丁文改譯為 twiggy fig。

附生與寄生
Epiphytic Plants & Parasitic Plants

2020 年 4 月 9 日的自由時報頭版有一則很吸睛的新聞，標題是：

寄生大茄苳樹
石斛蘭花瀑超夢幻

內文是：「天宮石斛蘭盛開時，粉色花朵會從附生的樹幹一串串垂墜而下，宛若瀑布傾瀉，又稱瀑布蘭或倒吊蘭，位於嘉義縣番路鄉下坑村台三線 283 公里處的「佳鄉庭園餐館」庭園 8 棵巨大茄苳樹寄生的天宮石斛蘭，近來花況大爆發⋯。」

標題寫「寄生大茄苳樹」，內文開始說是「附生」，第三行則又說「茄苳樹寄生的天宮石斛蘭」。天宮石斛蘭到底是附生 (epiphytic) 還是寄生 (parasitic)？

▲ 亞力山大椰子樹幹附生薜荔，共存共榮。

「寄生植物」與「附生植物」完全不同。寄生植物 (parasitic plant) 是指一種植物生長於另一種植物身上，並從宿主 (host) 攝取養分以維持生活，像菟絲子 (*Cuscuta* spp, dodder) 之類。寄生植物根部有特化的吸器 (haustorium/root-sucker)，會穿過宿主的組織以吸取水分及養分。附生植物 (epiphytic plant)，又稱著生植物，只是一種生長或依附在其他活體植物上的植物，它自己可行光合作用，會充分利用落雨、落葉、落塵等外部資源，不會吸取宿主身上的養分。像喜歡著生在樹幹上的薜荔 (*Ficus pumila*, climbing fig)，鳥巢蕨 (*Asplenium nidus*, bird's-nest fern) 等就是附生植物。

英文網站 Quora 上有關於附生與寄生有很簡潔的答覆：

What is the difference between parasitic and epiphytic plants?

An parasitic plant absorb the nutrition of the host plant to survive while the epiphytic plant do not absorb any sort of nutrients from the host plant. Parasitic plants harms the plant's growth, productivity and kills the host plant by making it deprived from nutrition and photosynthesis. While the epiphytic plants doesn't show any unnecessary harmful effects to the host plant. It just need some sort of physical support for survival.

▲ 附生樹幹生長多年的薜荔給從底部截斷，但薜荔仍鍥而不捨，重頭長起。

石斛蘭 (Dendrobium) 是喜歡生長、依附在樹幹或岩石上的蘭科植物 (epiphytic and lithophytic orchids)，天宮石斛蘭 (*Dendrobium aphyllum*, hooded orchid)，又稱兜唇石斛，不是寄生植物！

　　我在從事植物導覽、生態解說時，發現一般人往往把「寄生植物」與「附生植物」混為一談，把常見的附生植物薜荔當作寄生植物。許多公園、校園裡的大樹，如果有薜荔著生，常會給鏟除，就是誤以為它會吸取宿主養分而慘遭毒手。

　　台灣的科學教育表面看起來還不錯，學生歷年來參加 PISA 的成績表現，以數學最為亮眼，其次是科學，但那只是很會考試，真正落實在生活上的科學觀念，其實還有待加強。

▲ 本照片綠色五片小葉的植物係宿主虎葛（*Cayratia japonica*），又稱五爪龍，遭菟絲子寄生（陳文彬 提供）。

島榕，雀榕與纏勒
Twiggy Fig, Deciduous Fig, Strangling

島榕 (*Ficus virgata*) 和雀榕 (*Ficus subpisocarpa*) 是台灣常見的榕屬植物 (*Ficus* spp.)，它們懸垂的氣根一觸及地面，就會加速成長，成為支柱根，之後還會和本體的枝幹融而為一。運用這樣的策略，它們生長速度很快，很容易就長得比別的樹還高大粗壯。

島榕、雀榕生命力很強，處處都能生長，除了泥土，連屋頂、牆上或其他樹木的枝幹上也能著生。它們的果實會吸引麻雀、白頭翁 (Chinese bulbul)、綠繡眼 (Swinhoe's white-eye) 或紅鳩 (red collared dove) 等啄食，種子隨著鳥的排遺 (defecation) 散播，如果鳥糞 (bird droppings) 掉在別的樹上，就會逐漸包覆宿主 (host tree) 的樹幹，同時迅速往下紮根，與宿主競爭土壤裡的養分及水分，往上伸展枝葉與宿主爭奪陽光，叫做「纏勒」(strangling)。宿主若遭完全覆蓋，遮蔽陽光，無法行光合作用，就會給絞殺取代。絞殺過程的長短隨環境因素而異，快則數年，慢則數十年。

島榕的學名 *Ficus virgata* 意為「多枝榕」，因此英文俗名以 twiggy fig 為宜，以往有

▲ 圖 1 纏勒現象：台北台大校園舟山路口 島榕纏勒茄苳 (重陽木)（蘇恆隆 攝）

譯為 large-leaved weeping fig，太過冗長，且未見維基百科或國外其他英文圖鑑採用，宜採用 twiggy fig，俾與學名及其形態相符。

島榕 (*Ficus virgata,* twiggy fig) and 雀榕 (*Ficus subpisocarpa,* deciduous fig) are common species of strangling fig in Taiwan. They can become massive so easier and quicker than other trees. As soon as the hanging aerial roots of the branches of a strangling fig reach the ground, they grow faster and faster, becoming standing roots, sometimes several meters high, connecting the ground and the branches and eventually merging with the main trunk.

The small fruits of Ficus trees are favored by some birds and the seeds contained in bird droppings are often deposited in the branches of other trees. The Ficus then grows either regular roots or aerial roots that reach the ground. In the meantime, the Ficus is also growing upward toward the sun and spreading until it overtakes and kills the host.

▲ 島榕（引自 陳文彬《看見台灣原生植物》）

The time a strangling Ficus takes to kill its host tree varies and is dependent on environmental factors; it can be as little as several years or as many as decades.

雀榕 (*Ficus subpisocarpa*) 學名中的 *subpisocarpa*，意思是小豆，指它的果實像小豆。除了一般的雀榕全台可見外，還有一種較少見的大葉雀榕 (*Ficus caulocarpa*, Stem-fruited Fig)，In Greek, *kaulos* refers to the stem, while *karpos*' refers to the fruit; hence, the name *Ficus caulocarpa* means Stem-fruited Fig.

大葉雀榕主要分布在台灣南北兩端，種名 caulocarpa 中的 caulo 意思是 stem，carpa=fruit。大葉雀榕葉子較雀榕寬大，但果實反而較小，初結果時為白色，成熟時轉為黑色，一般雀榕的果實則為粉紅色。

▲ 雀榕（引自 陳文彬《看見台灣原生植物》）

薜荔與愛玉
Climbing Fig

薜荔（*Ficus pumila*, climbing fig）為桑科榕屬木質爬藤，果實為隱花果（syconium）。昆蟲會進入果實上之凹洞，吸取花蜜為它傳粉。種名（specific epithet）中的 *pumila* 意思是 dwarf, referring to the very small leaves of the plant。

楚辭〈山鬼〉篇：「若有人兮山之阿，被薜荔兮帶女蘿，既含睇兮又宜笑，子慕予兮善窈窕。」（她彷若立於山阿，披著薜荔，繫著女蘿，睨睍脈脈地笑著，戀慕地望著我，體態如此優雅。）

柳宗元「驚風亂颭芙蓉水，密雨斜侵薜荔牆。」（急風吹亂水中的荷花，密雨斜打在爬滿薜荔的牆上。）

毛澤東寫過七律《送瘟神》：「綠水青山枉自多，華佗無奈小蟲何！千村薜荔人遺矢，萬戶蕭疏鬼唱歌。」詩中「千村薜荔」即指瘟疫流行，千村荒廢，爬滿薜荔。

台灣常見校園及社區圍牆或樹幹上爬滿薜荔，四季常青，提供難得的景觀。可惜許多人誤以為薜荔爬滿整面牆會傷建築，爬滿樹幹會對樹有害，三不五時就把它斷根。台大校園、殷海光故居、泰順公園都常見把原本綠意盎然的薜荔從根部截斷。截斷不久就會一片乾枯，非常難看。

愛玉（*Ficus pumila* var. *awkeotsang*）是桑科榕屬植物，與薜荔頗為相似，為台灣特有亞種，拉丁學名前兩字與薜荔完全一

樣，後面的變種（variant）名稱 awkeotsang，意即「愛玉欉」。愛玉果實橢圓，全果有白色斑點，薜荔果實近球形，只有尾端有白色斑點。愛玉雌雄異株，雌果具豐富果膠（pectin）及果膠酯酶（pectinesterase），可製愛玉凍。果實皆可製作消暑飲料。《台灣通史：農業志》記載「愛玉」的由來：

> 道光初，有同安人某⋯往來嘉義，採辦土宜。一日，過後大埔，天熱渴甚，溪飲，見水面成凍，掬而飲之，涼沁心脾，⋯細視水上，樹子錯落，揉之有漿，以為此物化也。拾而歸家，以水洗之，頃刻成凍，和以糖，風味殊佳⋯某有女曰愛玉⋯，長日無事，出凍以賣，飲者甘之，遂呼為愛玉凍。（連橫，1921）

▲ 圖 1 薜荔（*Ficus pumila*）
（引自 陳文彬《新細說台灣原生植物》）

▲ 圖 2 愛玉（*Ficus pumila* var. *awkeotsang*）
（引自 陳文彬《新細說台灣原生植物》）

不過連橫所述「某有女曰愛玉……」，恐怕是牽強附會，台灣女孩其實很少叫「愛玉」的，不過名字中只要有一「玉」字，不管叫「寶玉」、「美玉」，一般都會暱稱「阿玉」，阿玉賣的果凍冰，轉寫而成「愛玉凍」、「愛玉冰」。

▲ 圖4 薜荔熟果及未熟果（鄭杏倩 繪）

都是麵包樹惹的禍
Breadfruit & *Mutiny on the Bounty*

麵包樹是桑科麵包樹屬（*Artocarpus*），與波羅蜜（*Artocarpus heterophyllus*）同屬，該屬植物多為雌雄異花同株，是全台灣各地都頗為常見的庭園樹木。屬名 *Artocarpus* 的 arto = bread, carpus = fruit，意思是「可作為糧食的果實」。

在台灣，麵包樹是阿美族的族樹，稱為 *Pacilo*（巴吉魯），傳說是阿美族的祖先乘木舟從海外帶回種植，在花蓮地區幾乎隨處可見，麵包果以花蓮的產量最多，品質最好。麵包樹果實含量

▲ 麵包樹的果實

豐富澱粉、醣類、蛋白質、纖維素、維他命等，鉀含量是香蕉的 10 倍，也含有鋅等礦物質。

中央研究院鍾國芳教授指出台灣的「麵包樹」學名應該是 *Artocarpus treculinus*，以往標示為 *Antrocarpus altilis*，其實是不同物種，那是引發「邦蒂艦叛變」(Mutiny on the Bounty) 的「太平洋麵包樹」。

台灣的「麵包樹」大概是由菲律賓傳進來的，學名中的小種名 *treculinus*，是為紀念法國植物學家 Auguste Trécul，他是桑科植物的專家。而「太平洋麵包樹」的小種名 *altilis*=fattened, fat, fed up for eating 意思是「有飽足感」。

遠征大溪地採集麵包樹苗

十八世紀末英國庫克船長 (Captain James Cook) 遠征太平洋探索，1769 年 4 月抵達位於大洋洲的大溪地，隨船植物學家班克斯 (Joseph Banks) 發現原住民稱為 'uru 的麵包樹是一種營養、好吃、易種的植物。那時大英帝國殖民西印度群島（British West Indies），希望能有供應當地奴隸食物的廉價來源，Banks 建議英國政府去大溪地採集麵包樹種苗，到英屬西印度群島去種植。

1787 年五月英國皇家海軍買了一艘運煤船，改裝後命名為邦蒂艦 (HMS Bounty)，英王任命曾經隨庫克船長出航的布萊（William Bligh）為艦長，任務就是到千里之外的大溪地去採集麵包樹種苗，結果卻引發叛變事件。

這艘船原本較大的船長室經過改裝，以便放置麵包樹種苗盆栽。也裝上玻璃窗，通到上層甲板以利採光。為節約用水，地板加鋪鉛板，以收集澆灌種苗滲流出來的水重複利用。船長改住到水手和軍官住宿區隔壁窄小的艙室。

1787 年 12 月 23 日，邦蒂艦載著 46 名船員，由 Spithead 出發，花了近 10 個月的時間，於 1788 年 10 月 26 日航抵大溪地。他們在大溪地採集了 1,015 棵麵包樹樹苗，停留島上五個月，待樹苗比較苗壯，以便船運。

邦蒂艦叛變 Mutiny on the Bounty

大溪地女人美麗大方，深深吸引船員們，大副 Fletcher Christian 娶了一個大溪地女人，許多船員也有女朋友。但 Bligh 和 Christian 的關係卻逐步惡化，Bligh 對船員們極其嚴苛，經常當眾指責 Christian，與其他船員的爭執也愈來愈多，一場叛變已悄悄的在醞釀。

1789 年 4 月 5 日，邦蒂艦載著麵包樹苗駛離大溪地。約 3 個星期後，發生叛變 (mutiny)，Christian 和 3 名船員潛入 Bligh 的臥室，以刺刀脅持 Bligh，船員中有 18 位加入叛變……

Christian 控制了邦蒂艦，把船長和忠於 Bligh 的船員趕進一艘七米長的備用支援船艇 (launch)，放逐海上。

布萊艱苦漫長的航行 Bligh's epic voyage

在沒有羅盤與海圖的協助下，布萊憑著一個六分儀 (sextant) 和一隻懷錶 (pocket watch)，歷經 6,500 公里、47 天的驚險海上旅程，於 1789 年 6 月 14 日抵達荷蘭殖民地帝汶 (Timor)，告知這次的叛變事件，休息兩個多月。再轉往雅加達搭船回國，終於 1790 年 3 月 14 日回到英國，報告這次的叛變事件。

根據這個歷史事件寫成的小說 Mutiny on the Bounty 多次搬上銀幕。1935 年由 Frank Lloyd 改拍成電影《叛艦喋血記》，贏得了當年的奧斯卡最佳影片，主角之一是克拉克·蓋博 (William Clark Gable)；1962 年 Lewis Milestone 又拍成同名的電影，得到當年奧斯

卡金像獎七項提名，主演之一是馬龍・白蘭度 (Marlon Brando)。不過中文片名刻意誇張，叛變的過程中並沒有造成死傷「喋血」。

潘朵拉號的最後航行

英國政府據報後、派遣一艘海軍軍艦 (HMS Pandora) 去尋找邦蒂艦及捉拿叛變份子，由船長愛德華帶領的潘朵拉號於 1790 年 11 月啟航，船員人數比平時多一倍，因為找到邦蒂艦後，要有一批船員來操作遭叛徒劫持的邦蒂艦。

潘朵拉號於 3 個月後抵達大溪地，拘捕了十名參與叛變的船員，關在臨時監房裡，船員們戲稱監房為「潘朵拉的盒子」(Pandora's box)。 潘朵拉號於 1791 年 5 月初離開大溪地，在附近找了 3 個月，但沒找到邦蒂艦及其他叛變船員。

潘朵拉號於返回英國途中，8 月 29 日在澳洲大堡礁外海觸礁，潘朵拉號沉沒，31 名船員和 4 名叛變者淹死。囚犯與其餘船員分別登上小船，駛向帝汶，於 9 月中抵達。

第二次尋找麵包樹之旅

在愛德華船長回英國之前，Bligh 已帶領另一批船員展開第二次大溪地採集麵包樹的旅程，於 1792 年把 2,000 多棵麵包樹樹苗及過百種其他物種帶到英屬西印度群島。

審判

10 名生還的叛變者回到英國後接受審判，叛變期間有否持武器的是治罪的決定因素。4 人宣判無罪、3 人有罪但獲特赦，其餘 3 人判處絞刑。

本文在修訂時做了不少補充及修正。譬如根據鍾國芳博士的研究，修正了麵包樹的學名為 *Artocarpus treculianus*。

▲Fletcher Christian and the mutineers seize HMS *Bounty* on 28 April 1789. Engraving by Hablot Knight Browne, 1841

　　學名中的小種名 *treculianus*，拉丁文詞典中找不到，Kew Garden 的 Plants of the World Online 也沒有說明。我推測也許是在菲律賓採集到麵包樹標本的美國植物學家 Adolph Daniel Edward Elmer，在新品種發表命名時向法國植物學家 Auguste Trécul 致敬，表彰他的貢獻。在更早之前，與麵包樹同科不同屬的 *Treculia* 屬，譬如 *Treculia Africana* (African breadfruit)，屬名也是以他的姓氏命名的。

西番蓮、百香果與毛西番蓮
Passion Flower & Stinking Passion Flower

　　百香果（*Passiflora edulis*, passion fruit/passion flower）中文正式名字叫「西番蓮」，原產熱帶美洲巴西、巴拉圭等地，17 世紀傳入歐洲，西班牙傳教士發現其花外形頗似基督釘在十字架出血形象，因此以 passioflos 名之，直譯為耶穌基督受難花（passion flower）。約 30 年前，水果商按西語、法語發音稱之為「百香果」。學名 *Passiflora edulis*，必須斜體，首字 *Passiflora* 是屬名（generic name），必須大寫，意即 passion flower，第二個字 *edulis* 是種小名（specific epithet），意思是 edible。

▲ 圖 1 西番蓮（余淑慧 提供）

▲ 毛西番蓮（引自 陳文彬《新細說台灣原生植物》）

　　百香果日治時代已引進台灣，因為花的外觀像鐘錶，花蕊像時針、分針、秒針，所以日文名為「時計草」（tokeiso），台語也稱之為「時計果」。英文仿西班牙文，因花冠正面像耶穌基督受難，釘在十字架上流血，所以叫 passion fruit/passion flower。常有人不知命名由來，說英文的意思是＊熱情果。根據 Merriam-Webster 大詞典，passion 的 5 個義項中，第一項是「基督受難」the sufferings of Christ，第四、第五才是「熱情」（intense, driving, or overmastering feeling or conviction; ardent affection）。

　　除果農栽培外，在野外也可見到歸化野生的百香果，如木柵、新店山區常可看到它的蹤跡。

　　中南部山野還常見一種原產熱帶美洲，也是西番蓮屬（Passiflora）的歸化植物，毛西番蓮（*Passiflora foetida*）Stinking Passionflower，又稱為小時計果、全株密生長毛。

西番蓮、百香果與毛西番蓮

115

毛西番蓮葉子揉碎具難聞的氣味，種名 foetida 就是 stinking 的意思。黃色漿果卵球形，由三片羽裂狀的苞片包裹著，夏初開花，夏末秋初結果。高雄西子灣山坡地上常見的攀爬植物。

Passiflora foetida (**stinking passionflower**) is a species of passion flower　The specific epithet, *foetida*, means "stinking" in Latin. When crushed, the leaves give off an unpleasant pungent odor.

▲ 圖 3 & 4 毛西番蓮（陳文彬 提供）

流蘇
Chinese Fringetree

　　流蘇 (*Chionanthus retusus*) 英文叫 Chinese Fringetree，是台灣原生種 (native species) 的木犀科 (*Oleaceae*, olive family) 植物。Olive family 是木犀科，不過在台灣的英語教學常把 olive family 誤稱為橄欖科，橄欖科英文是 torchwood family，學名是 *Burseraceae*。

　　流蘇學名第一個字 *chionanthus*，也就是屬名，是「雪花」之意，chion 意即 snow，anthos 是 flower。英文系的同學大概都讀過 Norton Anthology（諾頓文選），anthology 本義就是「名花薈萃」。學名的第二個字 *retusus*，是種加詞 (epithet)，是指葉先端鈍或略凹 (apex rounded or obtuse with a slight notch)。

　　原生流蘇樹分佈在北部角板山和桃園南崁溪沿岸，陽明山天溪園草原區旁的山坡地亦可見蹤跡。十多年前流蘇算是台灣較少見的樹木，所以台大校園的流蘇老樹就成為園藝商人偷剪枝條、扦插育苗的「母樹」，台大還曾因此立牌「不得盜剪」。

　　「流蘇」一詞在古代原本是指以羽毛或絲線製成的穗子，作為馬車、

▲ 流蘇（引自 陳文彬《新細說台灣原生植物》）

帷帳等之裝飾,後來引伸為仕女服裝,如披肩、圍巾的下擺,洋裝的邊緣裝飾,額頭下垂的頭髮,英文稱為 fringe。流蘇的花冠呈 4 深裂,裂片細長,望之有如白色流蘇,因而得名。

流蘇每年約三月底、四月初開花,白淨素雅,猶如覆雪,到八、九月時會結成紫黑色核果,可用來繁殖。近年來流蘇種得越來越普遍。台北市新生南路 3 段 36 號到 96 號之間,近年也種了一排作為行道樹。

美國也有一種與我們同屬不同種的「美國流蘇」(*Chionanthus virginicus*),英文叫 American Fringtree 或 White Fringtree,花與我們的流蘇很相似,但葉子沒鈍頭,葉緣也無鋸齒。

▲ 美國流蘇 Wikipedia （取自 Wikipedia）

從苦苓、苦楝到戀樹
Chinaberry Tree

　　楝樹 (*Melia azedarach*) 英文叫 Chinaberry tree 或 Pride of India，台語稱為「苦苓」，是台灣原生植物，每年三、四月開花。因其樹皮及果實味苦，故又稱「苦楝」。楝花淡紫，微香有若洋玉蘭 (southern magnolia)，成串的核果 (drupe) 成熟時淡黃，所以又叫金鈴子。春天剛開花時，有時可見到去年結的果與新開的花並存樹梢。

▲ 楝樹花果並存（鄭杏倩 攝）

Chinaberry tree (苦楝), also called Pride of India, is a species of deciduous (落葉) tree in the mahogany family (*Meliaceae* 楝科), native to Asia. Chinaberry trees are prized as shade trees and bear pale purple tube-like blooms with a heavenly scent much like southern magnolia (洋玉蘭) trees. The light yellow drupes (核果) are toxic to humans, but are enjoyed by birds. The leaves on top are dark green, and pale green below. The leaves make an obnoxious (惡臭) odor when crushed. (據 Can You Grow Chinaberry Trees 一文濃縮改寫)

宋人張蘊〈詠楝花〉詩「綠樹菲菲紫白香，猶堪纏黍予沉湘。江南四月無風信，青草前頭蝶思狂。」「紫白香」勾繪出楝花淡紫、微香的特色，「猶堪纏黍」是指它細細的枝條勉強可用來綁粽子。

席慕容的〈苦楝〉一文中有：「誰說植物世界是靜默的世界，在這一棵苦楝樹開花的時候，整個億載金城裡都聽得見春天歡呼的聲音！」；莊柏林的〈苦楝若開花〉歌詩：「苦楝若開花　就會出香味　紫色的花蕊　隨風搖 隨雨落」；陳耀昌醫師的歷史小說《苦楝花 Bangas》，即是以楝花作為象徵，Bangas 就是撒奇萊雅語楝花的意思。

賴明煌博士〈為苦苓叫屈〉(自由廣場，3/21/2022) 一文中提及「淡白紫緻、浪漫親柔之台灣原生苦楝花〈苦苓花〉，……不畏潮風鹹土，生長快速，……可防風抗旱，……台灣農村不喜種苦楝，……因諧音「苦苓、可憐、苦戀」的聯想所致，且民間……傳聞朱元璋【因】苦楝籽……砸其臭頭而詛咒「苦楝黑心死過年」。不知……能否設法將苦楝正名「台灣紫楝」，鬆解被詛咒惡名，讓國人與鳥雀蟲蝶皆歡喜！」

早年由於迷信，楝樹往往一長出來就遭砍除，有一段時間不太容易看到。近二三十年來生態觀念漸有改善，才又在野地大量出現。高速公路及未受干擾的路旁常可見到自生的楝樹，在三、四月初綻放美麗的花朵。台北市新生南路三段86號台北真理堂大門右方就有一棵大楝樹，每年春季開滿紫花。

2021年10月24日，我導覽〈紀州庵同安街 生態走讀〉，之後有場【想像同安街】文學 × 生態「共識凝聚」工作坊。座談中提到台北市政府計畫打造同安街為「文學之路」，由孫啟榕建築師負責整體規劃，打算在同安街沿途種植楝樹，但遭遇社區民眾抗拒，認為苦楝不吉祥。還有民眾表示，如果一定要種，「千萬不要對著我家！」

我想解決的方式是：以後就直稱「楝樹」，把「苦」字拿掉，在香港及中國大陸，他們就叫「楝樹」，也可重新包裝，稱之為「戀樹」(Love Tree) 來推廣行銷。

從台灣連翹到金露花
Duranta erecta

吳濁流有部小說叫《台灣連翹》，以這種植物來隱喻台灣人的處境與命運，他在更早《亞細亞的孤兒》書中有以下這段文字：

他一面賞玩無花果，一面漫步到籬邊，那兒的台灣連翹修剪得非常整齊，初生的嫩葉築成一道青蔥的花牆，他向樹根邊看看，粗壯的樹枝正穿過籬笆的細縫，舒暢地伸展在外面。他不禁用驚奇的目光，呆呆望著那樹枝，心想：那些向上或向旁邊伸展的樹枝都已被剪去，唯獨這一隻能避免被剪去的厄運，而依照她自己的意志發展她的生命。

吳濁流小說裡的「台灣連翹」指的原產墨西哥、南美的馬鞭草科植物 *Duranta erecta*, golden dewdrop，不是原產中國的木犀科「連翹」(*Forsythia suspense*, weeping forsythia)。

「台灣連翹」，台語叫「苦林盤」(khóo-nâ-puânn)，果實有毒。開淡藍紫色花、五瓣，花序成串下垂，結一串串金黃色露珠狀果實，因此英文叫 golden dewdrop，意即金黃色露珠。剛好 1950-60 年

▲ 金露花
(取自認識植物 http://kplant.biodiv.tw)

代有位家喻戶曉的美國電影明星叫金露華 (Kim Novak)，代表作是希區考克執導的《迷魂記》，園藝商人腦筋動得快，就把這種植物稱為「金露華」，「華」、「花」兩字相通，現在一般稱為「金露花」。

The genus name is in honor of Castore Durante, a fifteenth-century Italian botanist. The specific epithet erecta means "upright" in Latin. The plant is also known as Duranta repens, from the Latin for "creeping". The latter name was originally used to identify smaller-leaved varieties of the species.

金露花分枝細密，葉腋具銳刺，以往台灣農村及宿舍常種植來做圍籬 (hedge)。它要生長到一定高度才會開花，但現在校園及路旁的金露花樹籬，往往過度修剪 (over-pruned)，所以不容易看到它美麗的藍紫色花朵及金黃色果實。近年來也可見到園藝商人新引進、花色艷紫的「蕾絲金露花」(*Duranta erecta* cv. 'Lass')。

▲ 蕾絲金露花 *Duranta erecta* cv. 'Lass'
（取自高雄旅遊網）

註：之前我的臉書貼文金露花學名用是它的異名 *Duranta repens*，現修正為 *Duranta erecta*。以往金露花常見的學名是 *Duranta repens*，唯近年來植物學界大多採納 Gail Bromley 1984 年的考證，以最早見諸出版為原則 (priority of publication)，改用 *Duranta erecta* 正式名稱，*Duranta repens* 則作異名。在植物分類學 (taxonomy) 上，如果先後有好幾個學名，不是目前學界正式採用的，稱為異名 (synonym)。

話說鳳梨
Ananas Cosmusus

　　台灣產的鳳梨香甜多汁、風味濃郁，而且物美價廉，如果你在國外吃過鳳梨，或吃過進口鳳梨，你一定會覺得差很大。

　　鳳梨 (*Ananas comosus*) 原產於南美洲亞馬遜河流域一帶，1493 年哥倫布在加勒比海的瓜地洛普島 (Guadeloupe Island) 第一次看到鳳梨，隨後把它引進歐洲。(Christopher Columbus was the first person to introduce pineapples to Europe in 1493 after encountering it on Guadeloupe Island.)

▲ 鳳梨 Pineapple
（Angela Chuchen 攝）

　　鳳梨科植物的拉丁學名 Bromeliad/Bromeliaceae，是法國植物學家 Charles Plumier (1646-1704) 為了「表彰」一位無籍籍名的瑞典植物學家 Olaf Bromelius (1634-1705) 而命名的 (named after Olaf Bromelius, a little-known Swedish botanist)。Charles Plumier 是法王路易十四欽命植物學家，三度遠赴中南美洲加勒比海地區調查植物，緬梔 / 雞蛋花的屬名 *Plumeria*，就是以他的姓氏命名。Plumier 早 Bromelius 一年過世，當年他以 Bromeliaceae 命名鳳梨科的用意，是要向世人「表彰」Bromelius 的貢獻，「發潛德之幽光」，而不是「紀念」他。譯者在翻譯 "after someone" 時，不要千篇一律的譯為「紀念」，任意幫活人「作古」。

話說鳳梨

　　鳳梨英文叫 pineapple，是因為果實像松果，至於名稱裡的 apple 不是指蘋果，apple 在英文裡有時是水果的泛稱。不過根據文獻，在 1398 年，"Pineapple" 是指松樹的果實，後來松果改稱為 "Pine Cones"，由鳳梨 (*Ananas comosus*) 取而代之，稱為 "Pineapple"。(The name "Pineapple" was actually first applied to pine cones in 1398. Pine cones later took over as the common name, and *Ananas comosus* became known as the Pineapple due to its similar appearance.)

　　鳳梨 16 世紀末傳至中國，它的拉丁文是 bromelia，大陸及港澳截取 bro 之發音，稱作「菠蘿」。鳳梨在中國叫「菠蘿」還有一個原因，因鳳梨外表像由印度傳入中國，有千年歷史的波羅蜜 (*Artocarpus heterophyllus*) 。17 世紀天主教來華傳教士波蘭人卜彌格著作 *Flora Sinensis* (中國植物誌)，他筆下的「鳳梨」，寫為「反 (番) 波羅密菓子」。鳳梨台語稱為「王梨」，客語及馬、新一帶則稱「黃梨」。

　　一顆鳳梨其實是上百個小果聚合而成的。(A pineapple is not actually a single fruit, but hundreds of fruitlets that join together.) 鳳梨的植株密生螺旋狀排列的劍狀葉片，花序頂生，每一花序約有百餘朵紫紅色小花，長成聚合果，果實上的每一果目即是一朵小花長的小果 (multiple fruit consisting of coalesced berries)。聚合果頂端叢生緊密的小葉片，鳳梨學名 (*Ananas*

▲ A young pineapple in flower, from Wikipedia

comosus) 第二個詞 comosus，意即 tufted (成簇叢生的)，就是描述鳳梨果實的這種特徵。

鳳梨的果頂會著生「冠芽」(crown bud)，基部與果梗間會長「裔芽」(slip)，葉腋會長出「吸芽」(sucker)，莖基則有「塊莖芽」(tuber bud)，都可用來繁殖。鳳梨含有鳳梨酶 (bromelain) 是比木瓜酵素 (papain) 更強的、助消化的蛋白酶 (protease /ˈproʊtieɪz/)。因此若吃得太飽，幾片鳳梨很快就可化解。有人吃了鳳梨後舌頭會刺痛 (會咬舌)，有一種說法是鳳梨酶分解舌表面細胞的緣故，不過研究指出真正的禍首應該是果實中的草酸鈣 (calcium oxalate) 結晶形成的晶針 (raphides /ˈræfɪˌdiz/)。(The real culprit are raphides, which are calcium oxalate crystals.)

削好的鳳梨沾到水，果實中的草酸鈣會形成晶針，游離出

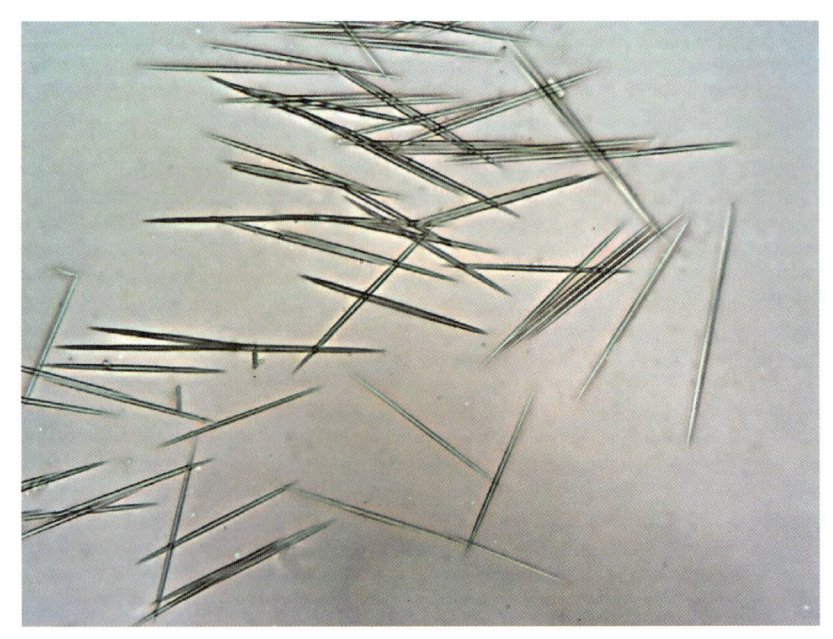

▲ Raphides /ˈræfɪˌdiz/ 晶針 (Wikipedia)

來，刺破舌頭、口腔黏膜，產生不適感。(raphides, needle-shaped crystals of calcium oxalate that occur in pineapple fruits and leaves, likely cause microabrasions, contributing to mouth discomfort.) 十幾年前果販削好鳳梨後會用水沖洗，現在賣鳳梨削好都不碰水，也是這個原因。

　　清康熙末，鳳梨由中國南方引進台灣栽培，迄今有300多年歷史。日據時代日本人在鳳山設立鳳梨工廠，開始製造鳳梨罐頭，1970年代台灣鳳梨罐頭的輸出曾執世界牛耳。近幾十年來台灣農業機構積極研究品種改良，培育出如金鑽鳳梨、牛奶鳳梨、蜜寶鳳梨、香水鳳梨等甜度、風味遠遠超越國外的鳳梨。

▲ 卜彌格 *Flora Sinensis* (中國植物誌)裡的「反(番)波羅密菓子」(鳳梨)

海芋與美人蕉
Calla Lily & Canna Lily

「海芋」與「美人蕉」的英文俗名很好記，也很像。海芋 (*Zantedeschia aethiopica*) 英文叫 calla lily 或 arum lily；美人蕉 (*Canna indica*) 英文叫 canna lily。我在 Tree Talk & Walk 導覽及上翻譯課時，提到海芋與美人蕉的英譯，常有人要我把它寫成文章。

美人蕉 (*Canna indica*) 是美人蕉科 (*Cannaceae*) 植物，原產於加勒比地區西印度群島，引進台灣已超過 350 年，花期很長，有紅、黃、橙紅等顏色。它像薑般的塊狀根莖發達，可用以繁殖，所以台灣民間婚嫁時常用來做為「早生貴子」的象徵，因此也是

▲ 圖 1 美人蕉 Canna indica（楊銘塗教授 提供）

▲ 圖 2 海芋與美人蕉（鄭杏倩 繪）

民俗植物。在物資缺乏的年代，它充滿蜜汁的花冠筒，可供吸吮，是鄉野間孩童的最愛。

網路上有人說美人蕉原產印度，係誤解學名 *Canna indica*，以訛傳訛的結果。其實學名裡的 *Canna* 是 cane 之意，因美人蕉的莖圓如桿；而 *indica* 則指西印度群島，而非印度。植物學家、鬱金香之父 Charles de l'Écluse (德萊克呂茲) 特別對命名做了說明：

Charles de l'Écluse, who first described and sketched C. *indica*, ... stated that it was given the name indica, not because the plant is from India, in Asia, but because this species was originally transported from ... the Western Indies.

另有校園、公園常見花朵較大的「大花美人蕉」(*Canna* × *generalis*)，則屬園藝雜交種，通常不會結果。

每年三四月陽明山竹子湖海芋 (*Zantedeschia aethiopica*) 花盛開，吸引不少遊客。海芋 (calla lily/arum lily) 原產於南非及非洲史瓦濟蘭等國，和芋頭 (taro)、姑婆芋 (giant elephant ear) 一樣是天南星科 (*Araceae*) 植物，中國大陸和香港則稱之為「馬蹄蓮」。

▲ 圖 3 海芋 *Zantedeschia aethiopica*
（取自 Wikipedia）

新興水果：黃金果與牛奶果
Abiu and Milk Fruit

　　台灣近年來引進不少新興水果，如黃金果、牛奶果等，但尚未普及。黃金果 (*Pouteria caimito*) 英文叫 abiu 或 caimito，在中國及新加坡稱為「黃晶果」，也有按種名 caimito 譯音，稱「加蜜蛋黃果」。黃金果是熱帶水果，原產南美，約 30 年前先後自新加坡及馬來西亞引入栽種。

　　Pouteria caimito, the abiu, is a tropical fruit tree originated in the Amazonian region of South America. Its fruits' shape varies from round to oval. When ripe, it has smooth, bright yellow skin and has one to four ovate（卵形）seeds. The inside of the fruit is translucent（半透明）and white. It has a creamy and jelly-like texture and its taste is similar to the sweet, caramel-like taste（焦糖味）sapodilla（人心果）with a

▲ 黃金果

smoother texture. The melting, sweet pulp (果肉) of the abiu is also used to flavor ice cream and cut into yogurt for a light and delicious breakfast. Abiu fruit is a significant source of calcium, phosphorus (磷), vitamin A, and vitamin C.

The abiu tree is part of the family *Sapotaceae* (山欖科) and is similar in appearance to the canistel (蛋黃果). (Adapted from Wikipedia)

黃金果完全成熟後果肉像果凍般半透明狀 (translucent and jelly-like)，可用湯匙挖取果肉食用 (scooping out the flesh with a utensil)，冷藏後食用口感更佳，也可添加在冰淇淋、優格或其他冰品裡食用。

黃金果與蛋黃果 (canistel) 同是山欖科桃欖屬，蛋黃果的種子煮熟可食，口感像栗子，但黃金果的種子含氰苷 (cyanogenic glycosides) 較多，不可食用。我原本以為既然是同屬，應該也可食，以神農嘗百草的精神試過一次，種子煮熟，仍然味苦，吃了舌頭有點發麻，經查英文文獻才知道曾有狗食用中毒的例子。

黃金果是山欖科桃欖屬，但在「認識植物」網站上 (Kplant.biodiv.tw) 卻誤植為 *膠木屬 (Pouteria)，膠木屬學名應為 *Palaquium*。

牛奶果 (*Chrysophyllum cainito*)，牛奶果學名第一個字 *chrysophyllum*，意思是金葉，第二個字 cainito 意指胸乳，英文叫 milk fruit，原產巴拿馬，是台灣較少見的新興水果。稱為牛奶果的原因是切開後果皮會滲出白色乳汁，果肉呈乳白、半透明狀。牛奶果葉子背面金黃，果實暗紫色，扁球形，橫切面放射星芒，因此又叫 star apple，中國大陸稱「金星果」。英美人士往往在不熟

悉的水果後面加上 apple 一詞，意思是「（水）果」的泛稱，有人把 star apple 按字面直譯為 *「星蘋果」，其實是不正確的。

臺灣的牛奶果是從越南引進，高雄六龜、美濃一帶種植較多，每年的 1-5 月是產季。牛奶果食用時最好用湯匙挖，若直接剝開食用，果皮上的乳汁容易黏在嘴唇上。

Chrysophyllum cainito is a tropical tree of the family *Sapotaceae* (山欖科). It is native to the Isthmus of Panama 巴拿馬地峽, where it was domesticated. It is now grown throughout the tropics, including Southeast Asia. The fruit has numerous names. The common name cainito likely come from Mayan. It is also called star apple, purple star apple, golden leaf tree, milk fruit. In Taiwan and Hong Kong, it is called "牛奶果", and in China, it is called "金星果".

▲ 牛奶果

檸檬與萊姆
Lemon & Lime

檸檬 (lemon)、萊姆 (lime) 都是芸香科柑橘屬的水果 (citrus)，它們都是酸而多汁 (juicy and acidic)，在台灣我們的檸檬幾乎都是綠色的，但在西方則幾乎都以黃色的樣貌出售。

臉友 Sc Chang 指出，在美國和加拿大的超級市場，綠色的檸檬一律標為 lime，lemon 則是專指黃色的品種，跟我們不一樣，lime 是綠色的，lemon 是黃色的，美國人就這樣認定。

其實 lemon (*Citrus limon*) 與 lime (*Citrus latifolia*, Persian lime 或 *Citrus aurantiifolia*, Key lime) 的差異跟顏色無關。一般來說，檸檬比較大顆，呈橢圓形，果實外皮較厚、較粗糙，底部明顯突出 (oblong shape with a protruding end at the bottom)，而萊姆比較小，

▲ 檸檬

▲ 萊姆

外表圓形，果皮較光滑且薄，底部尖突不明顯。許多美國人以為外皮綠色的就是 lime，黃色的就是 lemon，其實是不正確的。

台灣栽種的檸檬品種和西方一樣，主要都是「優列喀」(Eureka) 品種，全年皆產，但以 7-8 月為盛產期。台灣以往很少種萊姆，現在開始有種植 Persian lime，卻把它稱作「無子檸檬」。

台灣的檸檬果皮顏色和國外不一樣，是因為氣候不同所造成的。在溫帶地區，檸檬還未採收前顏色就已經變黃了，在台灣則 7-8 分熟時還是綠色，全熟才會變黃。西方地中海比較溫暖地區的檸檬果皮就不那麼容易變黃，果農會迎合消費者的心理，把檸檬催熟，讓果皮變黃後再販售。

語言反映我們對周遭事物的認知，不過只能反映一般庶民的認知，和專家的認知有時會有一些差距。

橘子與橙
Tangerine & Orange

一般而言 orange 指「橙」，我們稱作「橘子」的，通常是 tangerine (*Citrus tangerina*) 或 mandarin orange (*Citrus reticulata*) 之類的栽培雜交種。英文 tangerine 的由來是因為英美人最早接觸到這種柑橘類是來自摩洛哥的 Tangier。英文 citrus 則指所有的「柑橘屬水果」，還包含檸檬 lemon、萊姆 lime、柚子 pomelo、葡萄柚 grapefruit 等。「柑橘園」英文可譯為 orange orchard。

英美人比較少吃橘子，不太在乎橘子與橙的區別。因此早期大部分的英文詞典裏 orange 與 tangerine 的定義幾乎一樣。二十多年前我跟英美主要詞典出版社提出 orange 與 tangerine 有很大的不同：「橘子」皮較鬆，可輕易剝開 (with a loose skin that is easily removed)；「橙」外皮堅韌 (with a tough rind)，須用刀切。後來 Oxford、Longman、Macmillan 及 *Merriam-Webster Advanced Learner's Dictionary* 都修改了 orange 和 tangerine 的定義，基本上就是採納我的建議。

Orange 在中國大陸及港澳都叫「橙」，但在台灣卻有「柳丁」的特殊講法。華裔園藝家劉錦濃於 20 世紀初培育出耐寒抗霜的甜橙新品種，於 1914 年獲獎，名為「劉錦濃橙」(Orange Lue Gim Gong)，簡稱「劉橙」(Lue Orange)。因為「劉」、「柳」音近，「劉橙」傳到台灣，一般人不知其緣由，稱之為「柳橙」。又因台語把「橙」唸成「丁」，加上筆畫少，因此就產生了「柳丁」

這種特有講法。

華美文學名著 Wooden Fish Songs《木魚歌》，即是 Ruthanne Lum McCunn（林露德）以劉錦濃的一生及他和三位女子的故事為背景撰寫的小說，馮品佳教授中譯，書林出版。(http://www.books.com.tw/products/0010628108)

順帶一提，柑橘不用剝皮就可以知道裡面有幾瓣果瓣，只要把蒂頭剝掉，看看有多少小圓點就代表有幾瓣果瓣。9 個細點就有 9 瓣果瓣，11 個細點就有 11 瓣果瓣，依此類推。（可參見培養科學核心素養的科普童書《阿德老師的科學教室 4》植物大搜密，信誼出版）

▲《木魚歌》

▲ 橘子剝掉蒂頭後看細點即可得知果瓣數

阿勃勒、台灣欒樹、金鍊花
Golden Shower Tree, Taiwan Golden Rain Tree, Golden Chain

　　從初夏 5 月起，「阿勃勒」(*Cassia fistula*) 就開始綻放花朵，一直到 8 月，盛花期滿樹垂掛一串串的金黃色的花朵，飄落遍地的花瓣，有如下過一陣豪雨，因此英文叫 golden shower tree，台灣有人稱之為「黃金雨」，其實應該叫黃金「豪」雨。真正的「黃金雨」指的是「欒樹」(*Koelreuteria paniculata*, golden rain tree) 及「台灣欒樹」(*Koelreuteria elegans ssp. formosana*, Taiwan golden rain tree)。阿勃勒是臘腸樹屬，屬名 *Cassia* 指樹皮芳香，種名 *fistula* 是 "tube, pipe"，指果實管柱形。

　　每年 8 月底、9 月初，是真正黃金雨「台灣欒樹」登場的時候。金黃色的花開始綻放，圓錐花序 (panicle) 簇生樹頂；到了 10 月就結成磚紅色果的蒴果 (capsule)，粉紅或磚紅色的燈籠狀果實相當耀眼，由三瓣片合成 (a three-lobed inflated papery seed pods)。常常可見一棵樹上黃色的花和紅色蒴果同時並存。「欒樹」中國、韓國皆有，但「台灣欒樹」是台灣的特有亞種 (endemic subspecies)。

▲ 靜修女中前的阿勃勒 Golden Shower Tree（本書作者 攝）

137

▲ 台灣欒樹（Taiwan Golden Rain Tree）入秋後蒴果會轉為褐色（鄭杏倩繪）

阿勃勒是台灣師大的校花，泰國的國花，詩人余光中有詩〈詠阿勃勒〉：

「一盞盞，一串串，多少燦爛的金吊燈，初夏就這麼隨隨便便地，掛在行人的頭頂，害得所有的眼睛，驚喜中所有仰望的眼睛，像飛進童話的蜜蜂一樣，都恍惚迷路了。」除了余光中以外，還有向陽、陳義芝、呂自揚、汪啟疆、李魁賢等數十位詩人寫詩歌詠阿勃勒。

阿勃勒原產於印度、巴基斯坦、斯里蘭卡等地，中國古籍稱「阿勒勃」或「波斯皂莢」。「阿勒勃」為梵語 āragvadha 的音譯，台灣稱「阿勃勒」可能是把它與「金鍊花」(Laburnum, golden chain) 混為一談，金鍊花學名 Laburnum 發音很接近「阿勃勒」。金鍊花是原產法國南部到巴爾幹山區的有毒植物，乍看之下和阿勃勒的花很像（見圖）。阿勃勒的葉子是偶數羽狀複葉，每葉有 4-8 對小葉片，金鍊花的複葉則是三個小葉片 (leaves are trifoliate)。

▲ 金鍊花 Golden Chain (By J.F. Gaffard)

    Laburnum, sometimes called **golden chain**, is a genus of two species of small trees in the subfamily Faboideae of the pea family Fabaceae. The species are *Laburnum anagyroides*—**common laburnum** and *Laburnum alpinum*—**alpine laburnum**. They are native to the mountains of southern Europe from France to the Balkans.

    1980之前阿勃勒在台灣並不普遍，後來園藝景觀業者陳義男發現台灣師大有那麼吸睛的花樹，就來採種育苗推廣，所以台師大正門旁的幾棵阿勃勒是台灣許許多多阿勃勒的母樹。因為阿勃勒是台師大的校花，台師大畢業的校友也很自然喜歡在自己任教或主持校務的學校裡栽種，現在全台各地的校園、公園裡都不難看到它的芳蹤。

台灣欒樹
Taiwan Golden Rain Tree

「台灣欒樹」（*Koelreuteria elegans* ssp. *Formosana*）的英文叫做 Taiwan golden rain tree，每年九月起開始綻放黃色的花，圓錐花序（panicle）簇生樹頂；到了十月就結成磚紅色的蒴果（capsule），由粉紅或磚紅色的三瓣片合成像燈籠狀（a three-lobed inflated papery seed pods），相當耀眼。常常可見一棵樹上黃

▲ 台灣欒樹　樹上可見燈籠狀的蒴果。（蘇恆隆 攝）

色的花和紅色蒴果同時並存。

原產在黃河流域和長江流域下游的欒樹（*Koelreuteria paniculata*），已在韓國、日本歸化，現在世界各地皆有栽植，英文叫 golden rain tree。種名 paniculata means 'tufted'，意指花序簇生樹頂。

Koelreuteria paniculata is a species of flowering plant in the family Sapindaceae, native to China. Naturalized in Korea and Japan since at least the 1200s, it was introduced in Europe in 1747, and to America in 1763, and has become a popular landscape tree worldwide. (Wikipedia)

▲ 苦楝（蘇恆隆 攝）

「台灣欒樹」（*Koelreuteria elegans* ssp. *formosana*）則是台灣的特有亞種（endemic subspecies），它的屬名（genus name）欒樹屬（*Koelreuteria*），係紀念德國植物學家 J. G. Kölreuter 而來的，The genus was named after Joseph Gottlieb Kölreuter。屬名 *Koelreuteria* 發音 /kɛlrʊˈtɪəri/，種名 elegans 意指優美、吸睛，*formosana* 指台灣。

▲ 台灣欒樹

▲ 台灣欒樹磚紅色的蒴果

「台灣欒樹」葉形頗似苦楝（*Melia azedarach*, Chinaberry tree），因此台語又稱「苦楝舅」。不過「台灣欒樹」是無患子科（Sapindaceae），「苦楝」則是楝科（Meliaceae）。如無花或果實可供辨識時，可從新葉判斷，「台灣欒樹」新長的嫩葉帶著微紅，小葉互生（leaflets are alternate）。苦楝的嫩葉無論多小，都是綠的，小葉對生（leaflets are opposite）。

▲ 小葉互生的台灣欒樹

▲ 小葉對生的苦楝

辛夷 / 紫玉蘭與木芙蓉
Magnolia liliiflora & Hibiscus mutabilis

辛夷 (*Magnolia liliiflora*)，又叫紫玉蘭，花形很像洋玉蘭，都很碩大，但葉子則很不一樣。

台師大文薈廳前，沿著紅樓有 12 棵辛夷，標示牌寫「紫玉蘭」，三月時會花開滿樹，但葉子都掉光。有些植物在冬天葉子會掉光，天氣一轉暖，花開滿樹，花謝後，開始長葉，櫻及辛夷都有這種先花後葉的現象，但與辛夷同是 *magnolia* 屬的洋玉蘭就沒有這種現象。

美國 LA 常見的 magnolia 大多是洋玉蘭 (*Magnolia grandiflora*)，花更大，乳白色，花瓣較圓，辛夷花瓣則稍窄些。

網路上《古話今談》有人解說王維的《辛夷塢》一詩：「木末芙蓉花，山中發紅萼，澗戶寂無人，紛紛開且落。」，白話解釋：

「深山中有一株木芙蓉，枝頭上綻放著美麗的紅色花朵。儘管澗水邊的小屋裡靜寂無人，它依然不斷地盛開，也不斷地凋落。」

▲ 辛夷

但這則解說第一句就弄錯了,王維這整首詩是在歌詠「辛夷」,「木末芙蓉花」指的是「樹梢長著像蓮花一樣大而美麗的辛夷花」,不是一株錦葵科「木芙蓉」(*Hibiscus mutabilis*),見圖。古文/古詩裡「芙蓉」通常係指「蓮花」或「大而美麗的花」。蓮花即荷花,成語「出水芙蓉」即是以蓮花比喻出浴的美人,辛夷又稱木蓮,也是這個緣故。

▲ 木芙蓉(陳文彬 提供）

馬拉巴栗
Malabar chestnut

馬拉巴栗 (*Pachira aquatica/Pachira glabra*) 原產中南美洲沼澤地區，中文名稱來自英文 Malabar chestnut，俗稱發財樹、招財樹、美國花生，香港叫瓜栗，是錦葵科植物 (*Malvaceae*, mallow family)。一般中文介紹資料多把馬拉巴栗歸於木棉科 (Bombacaceae)，不過 2003 年的 APG II 分類法已把木棉科併入錦葵科。

馬拉巴栗四月中、下旬開碩大的花，花朵受孕成功後，像把小刷子的雄蕊 (stamen) 就會脫落。這些掉落的花蕊是美味的食材，加入排骨湯裡煮還挺不錯。七月起是果實成熟的季節，它的蒴果 (capsule) 成熟後果皮會迸開成五裂掉落，裡頭有十幾粒棕色圓形

▲ 馬拉巴栗的葉子及蒴果

▲ 馬拉巴栗的雄蕊

種子會散落出來。我們社區裡馬拉巴栗的種子通常都是我在撿拾 / 食 (forage)。種子泡水 12 小時後，種皮會裂開萌芽 (germinate)，用烤箱烤五六分鐘就是無上美食，口感像栗子與花生的綜合。

以下中英文係根據 Wikipedia 節改，可供 CLIL 教學參考：

馬拉巴栗為常綠喬木，樹皮綠色，幹基部常膨大。掌狀複葉，小葉長橢圓形 5-9 枚，花乳白色。蒴果像棵大鵝卵，球形種子褐色。常栽作為室內觀葉植物，種子可食用，樹幹可製紙。據南韓農業單位研究發現，馬拉巴栗能減少室內一半以上細懸浮微粒 (fine particulate matter)。

1986 年韋恩颱風來襲，台灣貨櫃車司機王清富，在家中幫從事美髮工作的太太編辮子。一時靈感，把五棵馬拉巴栗幼苗的枝幹紮成辮子狀，種在同一盆子，命名為「發財樹」出售，傳至日本，受到熱烈歡迎，成為東南亞最普遍的觀賞植物之一。在華人社會，這種植物象徵財運，有時更在樹枝上綁上紅絲帶等象徵吉祥的妝飾。馬拉巴栗在台灣有很重要的經濟地位，2005 年的出口值達 2 億 5 千萬新台幣。

▲ 切開後的馬拉巴栗蒴果與種子　　▲ 烘烤後的馬拉巴栗種子

嚴格說來，台灣目前廣泛種植的馬拉巴栗並非果實棕色的 *Pachira aquatica*，而是 *Pachira glabra*（光瓜栗）。

Pachira aquatica is a tropical wetland tree in the mallow family *Malvaceae*, native to Central and South America where it grows in swamps. It is known by the nonscientific names Malabar chestnut, French peanut, Guiana chestnut and Provision tree. It is commercially sold under the names Money tree and Money plant. This tree is sometimes sold with a braided trunk and is commonly grown as a houseplant.

The genus name *Pachira* is derived from a language spoken in Guyana. The species name is Latin for "aquatic." It is classified as part of the family *Malvaceae*. Previously, it was assigned to Bombacaceae.

In East Asia, *Pachira aquatica* (馬拉巴栗) is often referred to as the "shake money tree" (搖錢樹). This tree has long been popular as an ornamental in Japan. In 1986, a Taiwanese truck driver first cultivated five small trees in a single flowerpot with their trunks braided. The popularity of these ornamentals took off in Japan and later much of the rest of East Asia. They are symbolically associated with good financial fortune and are typically seen in businesses, sometimes with red ribbons or other ornamentation attached. The trees play an important role in Taiwan's agricultural export economy with exports of NT$250 million in 2005. However, many specimens in cultivation sold as *Pachira aquatica* are actually a similar species called *Pachira glabra*, which develops a thick base at a younger age and has a smaller growth habit, less showy flowers, and a 6" green seed capsule rather than 12" brown seed capsule.

蓮霧，釋迦，粉介殼蟲
Jambu/Champoo, Sweetsop & Mealybug

　　蓮霧、釋迦都是深受歡迎的台灣水果，2023 年中國海關總署突然發布通知，指台灣外銷的釋迦及蓮霧檢出介殼蟲「大洋臀紋粉蚧」，決定暫停輸入。粉蚧 (mealybug)，台灣叫粉介殼蟲，一般人多簡稱為介殼蟲。

　　蓮霧 (jambu/champoo, *Syzygium samarangense*)，又名洋蒲桃，星、馬稱作水翁，中、港、澳也稱作天桃，是桃金孃科蒲桃屬植物。學名中的種小名 *samarangense*，係因其模式標本採自印尼中爪哇的 Semarang (三寶瓏) 而得名。

　　蓮霧馬來語稱為 jambu air，第二個字 air 讀作 /ˈaɪə(r)/，是水的意思。荷蘭人把它從印尼引進台灣，音譯為蓮霧 lián-bū/lembu。以往蓮霧常見譯為 wax apple，聽起來好像素描靜物用的蠟製水果 (Wax Fruit)，曾有台灣人問美國朋友要不要吃蓮霧？Care for a wax apple? 對方回一句：Why not a real one? 我主張蓮霧按馬來語譯為 jambu，或近來美國市場流行的泰語講法，稱之為 champoo。蓮霧果實長得像鈴鐺，稱為 bell-fruit 也比 wax apple 高明。

　　以下中文摘自馬來西亞部落格「Ah Ying eh Blog - 阿盈的部落」：

> 水翁，我們檳城福建人稱 "水 jambu" (水翁原產於馬來群島，17 世紀由荷蘭人引進臺灣，由於我們稱 jambu，臺灣就音譯為蓮霧)，是我最愛的水果之一。

以下兩則介紹蓮霧的英文簡單明瞭：

Rose Apple, known in the U.S. market as champoo, is one of the most interesting exotic fruits in the world. …The fruit is hard to come by in Europe and America because of rapid deterioration (很快壞). It is also known as wax apple, water apple, bell fruit, water cherry, watery rose apple. (JAMBU AIR IN ENGLISH? http://englishchamberz.blogspot.com/2013/11)

The rose apple is yet another fruit with a surprise up its sleeve. Based on its outward appearance, it could easily be mistaken for a small pear, although the skin is usually quite waxy compared to pears. But when you cut the rose apple open, you won't find a core filled with seeds. The core of a rose apple is more or less hollow, with a bit of cottony fluff that should be scraped out and discarded.

Rose apples are eaten skin and all (帶皮吃). The texture is somewhere between a watermelon and an apple, as is the taste. (Rose Apples - Chompoo - Thailand For Visitors)

釋迦 (*Annona squamosa*) 原產於熱帶美洲，英文叫 sweetsop 或 sugar apple，但台灣學校裡學到的則是 custard apple。

Sweetsop/sugar apple is native to tropical climate in the Americas and West Indies. The Spanish traders of Manila galleons (馬尼拉大帆船) brought it to Asia.

Manila galleons 是 1565 至 1815 年間航行於中國、菲律賓與墨西哥之間的西班牙船隊，是他們把釋迦引入亞洲。釋迦 16 世紀傳到中國，因果皮似荔枝般有粒狀突起，故植物學上中文正式名稱

叫「番荔枝」。

在台灣,「釋迦」係荷蘭人自印尼引進,因印尼語為 srikaya,發音接近「釋迦雅」,加上果皮有突起鱗目 (a rind composed of knobby segments),似釋迦牟尼佛頭髻,所以台語稱之為「釋迦」。

釋迦樹高 3-5 公尺,枝細葉密。葉互生,正面深綠,背面灰綠。4 至 9 月開花,長橢圓形花瓣 3 枚,淺黃綠,散發濃厚果香。果實為聚合果,或稱集生果 (aggregate fruits),成熟果實呈淺綠或綠黃色,果肉乳白,口感綿密香甜,種子黑褐色橢圓形,光滑堅硬。

▲ 釋迦 Annona squamosa

▲ 鳳梨釋迦 Atemoya

「鳳梨釋迦」英文叫 atemoya，為傳統釋迦與秘魯釋迦之雜交種 (*Annona squamosa* × *Annona cherimola*)，1908 年於美國佛羅里達州人工雜交育成。The atemoya, *Annona squamosa* × *Annona cherimola* is a hybrid of the sweetsop and the cherimoya, both are native to the American tropics. Taiwan grown atemoya has the best quality – creamy and juicy!

馬來文裡傳統釋迦叫 buah nona，台灣改良的鳳梨釋迦品質超好，因此馬來西亞的果販特別幫它取個響亮的英文名字 Formosa nona，用以行銷。

致謝：謝謝李有成教授告知馬來語 jambu air 的 air 讀作 /ˈaɪə(r)/，是水的意思，nona 指釋迦這類的水果。

白千層
Weeping Paperbark

　　樹幹白色的「白千層」(*Melaleuca leucadendra*)，英文叫 Weeping Paperbark，樹皮像有千百層，極易剝離 (with flaky, exfoliating bark)，所以稱為「白千層」。它之所以演化出這種機制，是因為其原生地澳洲經常發生森林大火，當地叫 bush fire，而白千層的層層樹皮就是它的防火衣。它不怕火燒，反而很高興大火把其他樹燒死，自己就可稱霸天下了。它的種子經大火一燒，更容易萌芽，燒死的其他樹木的骨灰更成為它的肥料。白千層七月及十月時會開滿樹白花，花像小奶瓶刷，花粉有毒，敏感者吸入會造成過敏反應。

　　白千層學名 *Melaleuca leucadendra*，屬名 *Melaleuca*，意思是「黑」(*mela*)、「白」(*leuca*)，因為大火燒過後樹幹呈現有黑

▲ 白千層 *Melaleuca leucadendra*

有白的樣貌；種名 (specific epithet) 的意思是白樹。The specific epithet (*leucadendra*) is derived from the Ancient Greek words (leukós) meaning "white" and (déndron) meaning "tree", referring to the white bark of this plant.

現在流行的所謂「澳洲茶樹精油」(tea tree oil)，和茶樹毫無關係，它是白千層的近親，學名 *Melaleuca alternifolia* 的「細葉白千層」(Narrow-leaved paperbark) 葉子提煉的。*Melaleuca alternifolia*, commonly known as tea tree, is a species of tree in the myrtle family, *Myrtaceae*. (Wikipedia)

在澳洲，白千層俗稱 Ti Tree 或 Tea Tree，商人將之直譯為「茶樹」，不明就裡的人會誤以為就是我們平常所喝茶的茶樹。

▲ 細葉白千層 *Melaleuca alternifolia* by Geoff Derrin

松柏類樹木的英文
Conifer

　　松柏目樹木包括：松科、柏科、紅豆杉科、羅漢松科、南洋杉科等七科的針葉樹，其上位詞（總稱）是 conifer，以往的分類上的「杉科」現已廢除，併入柏科裡。

　　其下位詞（細稱）則有：

Conifers (Coniferae) 松柏類 comprise the following:

(1) pine family (Pinaceae) 松科: a. pine (Pinus) 松屬 b. fir (Abies) 冷杉屬 c. cedar (Cedrus), etc. 雪松屬等；

(2) cypress family (Cupressaceae) 柏科: a. cypress (Cupressus) 柏屬 b. juniper (Juniperus) 刺柏屬 c. false cypress (Chamaecyparis) 扁柏屬; d. Taiwania (Taiwania) 台灣杉屬 b. China fir (Cunninghamia) 杉木屬 c. bald cypress/swamp cypress (Taxodium), etc. 落羽杉屬等。

(3) yew family (Taxaceae) 紅豆杉科

(4) araucaria family (Araucariaceae) 南洋杉科

(5) yellow-wood family (Podocarpaceae) 羅漢松科, etc.

Note: the former 杉科 (Taxodiaceae) plants such as *Cunninghamia*, *Sequoia*, *Metasequoia*, *Taiwania*, and *Taxodium* are now grouped in the following subfamilies within the larger Cupressaceae: Cunninghamioideae, Sequoioideae, Taiwanioideae, Taxodioideae, etc.

別再炒作落羽杉
Say No to Bald Cypress

　　近年來一到秋天，媒體就開始炒作落羽杉，「全國最浪漫落羽松秘境…已開始褪下綠衣逐漸轉黃、變紅，呈現漸層美感…美如世外桃源」，「近年來落羽松的鋒頭逼近楓樹了。」觀旅局也推波助瀾，表示「泰安派出所…落羽松森林宛如人間仙境可以拍照打卡。」甚至台北大安森林公園生態池前幾年也重新改造，廣植落羽杉，缺乏生態環保意識，令人憂心。

　　由於商業炒作，近年來國內庭園造景一窩蜂搶種溫帶植物「落羽松／落羽杉」，沒有考量到任意栽種可能會造成環境災難。過去外來種的動植物危害自然生態的例子不勝枚舉，像是植物類的「銀合歡」(white popinac)、「小花蔓澤蘭」(mile-a-minute weed)，動物類的「福壽螺」(golden apple snail)、「巴西烏龜」(red-eared slider)、「琵琶鼠魚」(suckermouth catfish) 等，大家都耳熟能詳。

　　「落羽松／落羽杉」(*Taxodium distichum*)，在分類學上屬於柏科的落羽杉亞科 (Taxodioideae)，所以應叫「落羽杉」，英文稱為 bald cypress/swamp cypress，原生美國東南部沼澤地區，但適應力很強，若是種植在池塘或沼澤還好，但台灣多種在平地、庭園、路旁，只要水分充足，幾年後樹木周遭的地面就會冒出大大小小的膝狀根，高五至五六十公分不等，像鐘乳石筍，也像人的膝蓋，英文叫 cypress knee。往往造成周遭其他植物難以生存，不僅破壞生態，甚至會絆倒行人。

▲ 落羽杉周遭地面冒出的膝狀根

　　「落羽松 / 落羽杉」bald cypress/swamp cypress (*Taxodium distichum*) is a deciduous conifer in the family Cupressaceae. It is native to the southeastern United States. Hardy and tough, this tree adapts to a wide range of soil types, whether wet, dry, or swampy. It is noted for the russet-red fall color of its lacy needles (以紅褐色羽葉的秋色著名). (Wikipedia)

　　其實台灣每六到十年，商人為了商業利益都會大力推廣外來種的植物，媒體也往往推波助瀾，造成一時轟動。大家一窩蜂種植外來種植物，卻忽略這些植物可能對生態造成危害。一旦泛濫成災或價格崩盤，這些植物就遭拔除，任意丟棄。外來種植物不管被丟棄、種子隨風飄散、或隨鳥獸的排遺散播，如果在野外適應良好，就會變成入侵種 (invasive species)。強勢的入侵植物，遠

的如「馬纓丹」(lantana)、「布袋蓮」(water hyacinth)、「銀合歡」(white popinac)、「非洲鳳仙」(impatiens)，近的如「小花蔓澤蘭」(mile-a-minute weed)、翠蘆莉 (ruellia) 等，造成生態破壞都遠非引進外來植物之時所能預料的。

▲ 馬纓丹（蘇恆隆 攝）

以近年來農政單位、生態保育單位最頭痛的「小花蔓澤蘭」為例，它生長速度極快，所以英文叫做 "mile-a-minute weed"，它種子的繁殖能力很強，而且蔓莖接觸土壤的每個節都可長出根及芽，甚至節間亦能長出不定根 (adventitious root)，以營養體行無性繁殖 (asexual reproduction)，難以徹底根除。事實上，當初引進小花蔓澤蘭，竟是看重它繁衍速度快，可以很快達到綠化效果，為了水土保持，由有關單位引進，沒想到竟造成災難。據特有生物研究保育中心監測報告，2002 年小花蔓澤蘭蔓延危害面積超過五萬六千公頃，農業損失難以估計。以美國為例，2000 年學者估計入侵種造成美國的損失每年高達 1,370 億美元。

外來植物若造成危害，農業損失動輒以數十億、數百億計，但有時其後遺症 (after effects) 要在十年、二十年後才會顯現，因此我們在栽種諸如「落羽松／落羽杉」之類的外來植物時，必須審慎三思，不要盲目追逐流行，否則有可能成為破壞台灣生態的幫兇。

野薑花是古巴國花
White Ginger Lily

夏天是野薑花的季節，野薑的地下根莖（rhizomes）可作薑的替代品，像白色蝴蝶的花有股特殊的清香（Its scent is exquisite），可做插花，也可入菜。

野薑花 *Hedychium coronarium*, the white ginger lily, is a perennial flowering plant in the ginger family Zingiberaceae (薑科植物). It is native to the Eastern Himalayas of India, Bangladesh, Nepal and Bhutan, and even through northernmost Myanmar and Thailand, as well as southern China and Taiwan in the East. It is typically found growing in the forest understory (林下), where the pseudostems (假莖) arising from rhizomes (根莖) below ground may reach 1-3m in height. In its native environment, flowering occurs between August and December.

野薑花是古巴國花，在古巴叫 mariposa，意思是蝴蝶花。

The white ginger lily (*Hedychium coronarium*) is the national flower of Cuba, where it is known as **mariposa** (literally "butterfly") due to its shape.

野薑花並非古巴原產，古巴卻對它情有獨鍾，獨立後選為國花，是有原因的。

19世紀古巴對抗西班牙殖民的獨立戰爭中，往往透過女性身上或髮髻上插著野薑花，在花序的交錯的苞片縫隙裡夾藏字條，

幫助革命分子傳遞作戰情報。

Women used to adorn themselves with these fragrant flowers in Spanish colonial times. Because of the **intricate structure of the inflorescence** (繁複的花序構造), women hid and carried secret messages important to the independence cause under the inflorescence.

以下為古巴外交部對國花的說明：

The white mariposa (*Hedychium coronarium*) ⋯ became a symbol of Cuban flora because Cuban women used it to smuggle messages to the battlefield during the liberation wars of the 19th century. ("National Flower" Ministry of Foreign Affairs of the Republic of Cuba)

▲ 圖 1 野薑花 花序（鄭杏倩 繪）

野薑花的屬名 *Hedychium*，意思是芳香雪白，種小名 *coronarium*，意即皇冠。

The genus name *Hedychium* is derived from two ancient Greek words, *hedys* meaning "sweet" and *chios* meaning "snow". This refers to the fragrant white flower of the type species *H. coronarium*. Species epithet '*coronarium*' means 'crown'

近十年來語言教學提倡 Content & Language Integrated Learning（CLIL），多用這類有故事或知識內涵的材料來教學，學生應該會更感興趣。

▲ 圖 2 野薑花 花序（林國香 攝）

▲ 圖 3 野薑花 花開遍野（林國香 攝）

青花菜與花椰菜
Broccoli and Cauliflower

從十多年前開始，常見翻譯的文章把 broccoli（青花菜）譯為花椰菜，現在連本地出版品，甚至得獎的兒童讀物也把 broccoli 訛稱為 * 花椰菜或 * 綠色花椰菜！

根據 1987 年渡假出版的吳昭其《台灣的蔬菜（二）》一書（頁 62），以及農業相關部門：台灣省農會、台灣青果運輸合作社、台北農產運銷公司，早就把 broccoli 定名為「青花菜」。

2003 年農會出版郭人鳳《青花菜品種篩選與夏季栽培改進》，及 2005 年台南農改場出版謝明憲的專業報告《青花菜世代快速增進方法之建立》，都可見青花菜一詞才是正確名稱。

2003 年之後開始有譯者把 broccoli 誤譯為「花椰菜」，以致造成混淆。根據 Google Books，最早出現「* 綠色花椰菜」的出版品是 2003 年世茂出版的《三菜一湯的療效》（頁 113），該書顯然是根據英文資料編譯的。之後是 2007 年漢宇出版的《媽媽沒教的 1001 家常菜》（頁 33），書中把 cauliflower 和 broccoli 都稱為「花椰菜」，2008 年出版的一篇論文，則把 broccoli 稱為「* 綠花椰菜」。

花椰菜 (*Brassica oleracea* var. *botrytis*) 與青花菜 (*Brassica oleracea* var. *italica*) 都是十字花科 (Brassicaceae) 蕓薹屬 (Brassica)，雖然都是甘藍 (*Brassica oleracea*) 的變種，但外觀很不同。它們的種小名 *oleracea* 意思就是蔬菜。(Its specific epithet *oleracea* means "vegetable /herbal" in Latin.)

花椰菜花球通常是白色（現已研發出紫色和橘色品種），青花菜則是青綠色。花椰菜食用部位白色的花球是未分化的組織 (cluster of undifferentiated inflorescence meristems)，英文稱為 curd。青花菜食用部位綠色的花球則是已分化的花蕾 (clumps of densely packed flower buds)，花梗清晰可見，所以又稱青花苔，如果太晚採收，花蕾就會長成黃色的小花。（見圖 1 & 2）

Broccoli and cauliflower are strikingly different. Broccoli is green and you can look between its stalks, but cauliflower looks like a white solid mass wrapped in green leaves.

青花菜源於地中海義大利一帶，和花椰菜、球莖甘藍 (kohlrabi)、抱子甘藍 (brussels sprouts)、羽衣甘藍 (kale)、芥蘭 (Chinese kale) 同為甘藍 (cabbage) 的變種。Broccoli 一詞源自義大利文，意思是 flowering crest of a cabbage（甘藍開花的冠頂）；cauliflower 則來自拉丁文，意思是 the flowers of a cabbage（甘藍的花）。

▲ 圖 1 & 2 取自 Wikipedia

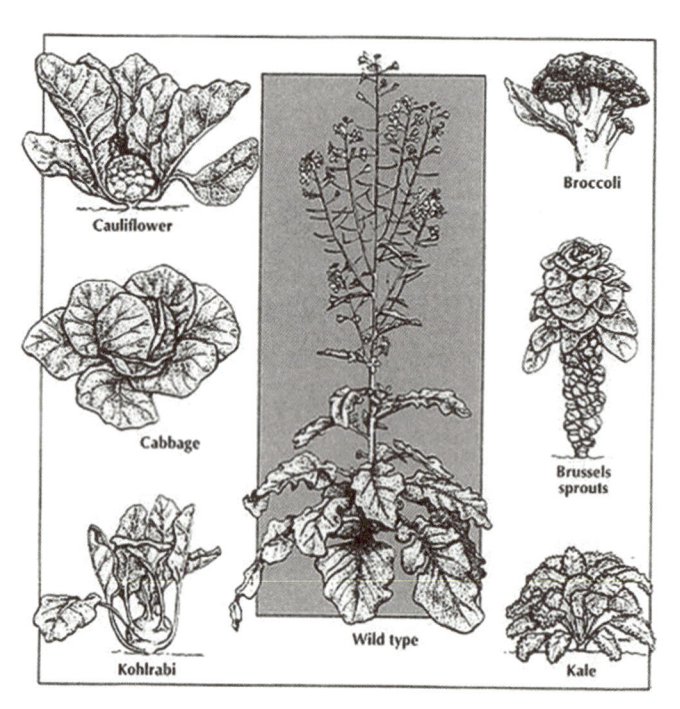

▲ 圖 3 中間為原始野生種甘藍 (wild cabbage, *Brassica oleracea* var. *oleracea*)，馴化成 6 大類外觀殊異的栽培品種 (cultivars)，圖取自 David R. Smyth, 1995.

　　青花菜在香港及中國大陸稱「西蘭花/西藍花」，因其產自西方，與同屬甘藍變種的芥藍味道相似，又像芥藍的花朵團簇，西方芥藍花，簡稱「西藍花」，藍、蘭同音，又訛轉為「西蘭花」。

　　花椰菜台語稱為「花菜」(hue-tshài/hue1-tshai3) 或「菜花」(tshài-hue)，17 世紀荷蘭時期就已引進種植。青花菜在二戰後才由美國傳入，但在 1975-1985 才大規模種植。1990 年 3 月媒體大幅報導：當時美國總統老布希在記者會上說，他從小就不愛吃青花菜，但小時媽媽會逼他吃，現在長大當總統，再也不吃了。之後，媒體又報導日本千葉大學研究，青花菜富含葉酸 (folate)，可預防

貧血、肺癌，從此青花菜就以抗癌 (anticarcinogenic) 蔬菜之姿流行起來。

On March 22, 1990, former president George H.W. Bush made an important announcement during a press conference. "I do not like broccoli, and I haven't liked it since I was a little kid and my mother made me eat it. And I'm president of the United States, and I'm not going to eat any more broccoli."

甘藍有許多變種，依食用部位概分為：花用甘藍（花椰菜、青花菜）、葉用甘藍（高麗菜、抱子甘藍、芥藍）、莖用甘藍（球莖甘藍）等，都屬於十字花科甘藍家族，英文統稱 the 'cole' vegetables。甘藍菜台灣俗稱「高麗菜」(ko1-le5-tshai)，很多人望文生義，以為源自高麗（韓國），其實應該是 cole, caulis 的音譯。

The 'cole' vegetables are grown and eaten throughout the world. They include such apparently diverse forms as cabbage, kale, brussels sprouts, kohlrabi, broccoli and cauliflower.

印度棗，中國棗，海棗 / 椰棗
Indian Jujube, Jujube & Date

每年二月前後正是又甜又脆的「印度棗」(Indian jujube) 盛產的季節，印度棗 (*Ziziphus mauritiana*) 果實綠色，原產印度、巴基斯坦。高雄燕巢地區 20 幾年前開始大量種植，經過改良，又甜又脆，果實比原產地的要大許多，是台灣冬季最受歡迎的水果。

有商人把它叫蜜棗，但這會引起混淆。因「蜜棗」原係指大陸進口的大棗蜜餞，是把大棗生果用割棗機周身割一遍，使得容易吸糖，然後入鍋用白糖煮，曬乾而成。

「中國棗」(jujube) 學名為 *Ziziphus jujube*，是溫帶的鼠李科 (*buckthorn*) 植物，原產中國、朝鮮半島。果實長圓形，未熟時淺黃綠色，成熟後褐紅色。可鮮食也可製成紅棗乾。現在苗栗地區也有栽種。

▲ 印度棗 (Indian jujube)　　　▲ 中國棗製成的紅棗乾

「黑棗」是加工品，係棗子加棉籽油和松煙水製成，所以不會看到「*新鮮的黑棗」。

「海棗/椰棗」(date) 學名為 *Phoenix dactylifera*，為棕櫚科植物，是中東國家的重要作物。沙烏地阿拉伯國徽兩把交叉彎刀的上方就是海棗樹。海棗的「海」是「洋」的意思，非指海邊，意指洋棗，外國棗。

兩年多前有學生問我：

蘇老師好：有個問題想請教老師。記得以前上課老師說過 date 是海棗，jujube 是棗子。近日譯書時出現一個句子，令我有點困惑……jujube 的用法已經積非成是了，那之後翻譯策略應該要怎麼辦呢？

我的回答是：常見誤譯與積非成是乃兩回事。兩種完全不同的水果不可能因誤譯就合而為一，植物學界更不可能接受。

幾十年來台灣英文課本和英漢辭典多把棗子誤為 date，但 20 多年前我初訪韓國時就注意到他們都寫 jujube。所幸台灣現在開始有改善的趨勢，最近我看水果行紙箱外的英文已印了 jujube，我在大賣場買的紅棗外包也是 jujube，可見我 20 年來的大聲疾呼，功不唐捐。

▲ 黑棗

▲ 海棗 (date)

▲ 蜜棗

印度棗，中國棗，海棗/椰棗

石榴，石榴石與音位/字位轉換
Pomegranate, Garnet & Metathesis

在超市見到美國加州進口紅通通的石榴，想起小時候讀過《千家詩》「五月榴花照眼明，枝間時見子初成。可憐此地無車馬，顛倒蒼苔落絳英。」（《千家詩》誤將此詩列為宋朱熹作，其實作者是韓愈。）

石榴 (Punica granatum) 原產中亞，相傳漢朝張騫從安西國帶回。晉人張華《博物志》記載：「張騫出使西域，得徐林安石榴以歸，故名安石榴。」元稹《感石榴二十韻》詩：「何年安石國，萬里貢榴花；迢遞河源道，因依漢使槎。」李商隱《茂陵》詩云：「漢家天馬出蒲梢，苜蓿榴花遍近郊。只待綠蔭芳樹合，蕊珠如火一時開。」都提到石榴的來源。不過山東農業大學陳興佳先生的論文「石榴的起源及其在中國的傳播」指出安西國、安石國，其實都是 Arsak（安息）的譯音。安息國，即西亞古國「帕提亞王國」(Parthia)，地處伊朗高原東北部。西班牙的格拉納達 (Granada) 以石榴得名，市徽上就有石榴。

石榴 (pomegranate) 和手榴彈 (grenade) 中文都有個「榴」字。英文 pomegranate 源自古法文 pomme-grenade，pomme 即 apple 或 fruit，grenade 即 seeded，意即「多子之果」，而更早的中古拉丁 pōmum = apple， grānātum = seeded 也是一樣。石榴和手榴彈除了形狀相似之外，落地都會爆開，both explode in a quite spectacular way!

英國有一家出版社叫 Garnet Education，以出版 ESP 聞名。除了石榴 (pomegranate) 和手榴彈 (grenade)，在中文與英文字源上都有關聯，garnet 這個字也一樣，在礦物上指「石榴石」，在顏色上指「榴紅」，（拜倒石榴裙下，「石榴裙」即「紅裙」），中文也都有個「榴」字。

英文 garnet 也是從石榴來的，是法文 *grenat*「換位」(metathesis) 的結果。語言學上在講音位／字位轉換時，常舉古英語 aks 變成 ask，brid 變換成 bird 為例，grenat 轉成 garnet 也是典型例子，就像中文與日文裡的「介紹」與「紹介」，普通話的「颱風」與台語的「風颱」。

新興蔬果：木鱉果
Gac Fruit

　　台灣人在吃的方面很勇於嘗試，喜歡嘗新，近年來又引進不少新興蔬果，最近 Joy Huang 老師在 FB 上 PO 出木鱉果的貼文及圖片，引起許多人好奇，我利用這個機會談一下幾種新興蔬果如木鱉果來龍去脈。

　　木鱉果 (*Momordica cochinchinensis*) 英文一般按越南語稱為 gac 或 gac fruit。Gac is a type of perennial (多年生) melon notable for its vivid orange-reddish color resulting from its rich content of beta-carotene (β 胡蘿蔔素) and lycopene (茄紅素). As gac originated in Vietnam, it is commonly called by its Vietnamese name "gac".

▲ 木鱉種子（黑）與苦瓜種子（白）

木鱉果學名第一個字 *Mormodica* 就是「苦瓜屬」，第二字 *cochinchinensis* 是「交趾支那」的意思，因標本是在越南南部的交趾支那 (Cochinchina) 採集到的。The species name cochinchinensis derives from the Cochinchina region in the southern part of Vietnam.

木鱉種子很像木刻的小鱉，因此得名，它和苦瓜 (*Momordica charantia*) 同一屬，所以種子形狀都很像，只是顏色、大小不一樣。（見圖）

木鱉果成熟時整顆橘紅，果肉可煮食，種子很大，外包覆一層紅色軟軟的假種皮，可以吮食，或挖出後放進罐子裡，加冷開水，用筷子攪拌，讓假種皮剝離溶解，加點糖、黑糖或蜂蜜、一點點塩、幾滴醋，就是很好的健康飲料。

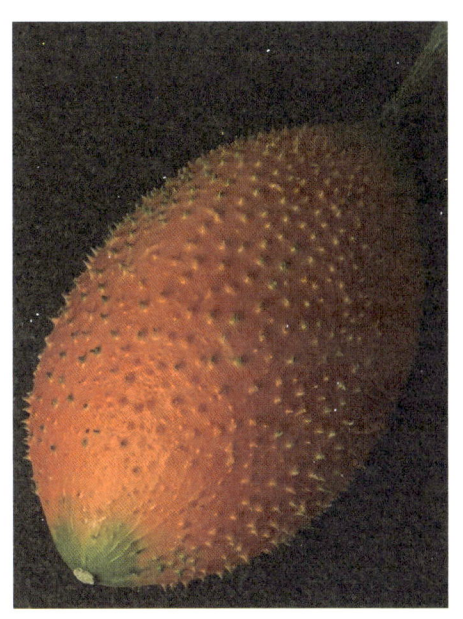

▲ 木鱉果（Joy Huang 教授提供）

▲ 切開木鱉果，露出外裹紅色假種皮的種子（Joy Huang 教授提供）

木鱉果的 β 胡蘿蔔素 (beta-carotene) 及茄紅素 (lycopene) 特別豐富，雖不是那種吃過會上癮的甜美蔬果，但可當它是健康食品，補充各種營養及微量元素 (trace elements). 底下是 2014 年《國際食品科技期刊》中一篇論文 "Gac fruit (*Momordica cochinchinensis*): A rich source of bioactive compounds and its potential health benefit" 的摘要。(December 2014, International Journal of Food Science & Technology)

Gac fruit has traditionally been used in Asia to provide red colour for cuisines and enhance visional health. Recently, Gac fruit has emerged as a potential source of carotenoids (類胡蘿蔔素), especially lycopene and β-carotene. Carotenoids and other identified bioactives (生物活性) from this fruit including phenolics (酚類化合物), flavonoids (類黃酮) and trypsin inhibitors (胰蛋白酶抑制劑) are associated with many beneficial bioactivities such as antioxidant (抗氧化), anticancer (抗癌) and provitamin A (原維生素 A) activities.

櫟樹、橡實、伊比利豬
Oak, Acorn, Iberian Pig

幾年前南下高雄演講，會後與昔日台大外文系的同窗聚餐。點餐時，店員特別推薦西班牙伊比利豬肉，並強調伊比利豬 (The Iberian pig) 是以橡實 (Acorn) 飼養，油脂分布均勻，帶有果香，風味有別於一般的豬隻。

Wikipedia 對伊比利豬簡介如下：

The Iberian pig is a traditional breed of the domestic pig that is native to the Iberian Peninsula (伊比利半島). The Iberian pig, whose origins can probably be traced back to the Neolithic (新石器時代), when animal domestication (馴化) started, is currently found in herds clustered in the central and southern part of Portugal and Spain.

一般人往往把 oak tree 誤譯為「橡樹」，其實是不正確的，植物學的名稱為「櫟樹」(*Quercus* spp.)，但是積誤已久，只好說俗稱「橡樹」。櫟樹的果實才叫「橡」或「橡實」(acorn)。臺灣的櫟屬樹木約有 20 種，最常見的是「青剛櫟」(*Quercus glauca*)，因為果實上有明顯的一圈一圈，所以英文叫 Ring-cupped Oak，全台從平地到 2000 公尺皆有分佈，為台灣黑熊的主食。

至於從櫟樹上掉下來的「橡實」(acorn)，如用來餵豬，則又稱為 mast。同一種東西，因不同成長階段、用途而有不同名稱的現象，在各種語言文化裡屢見不鮮。就像中文的「播稻」（台語 pòotiū-á），「插秧」，「割（刈）稻」，「曬穀」，「碾米」，

▲ 台灣黑熊主食「青剛櫟」Ring-cupped Oak 的「橡實」（李成華 攝）

「煮飯」，需用到 5 個不同的名詞，6 個不同的動詞，但稻、秧、穀、米、飯，英文概以 rice 稱之。

  Merriam-Webster Dictionary 對 mast 的解釋如下：

mast: nuts (such as acorns) accumulated on the forest floor and often serving as food for animals

  關於 acorn 一詞有不少俗諺，像 "like stealing acorns from a blind pig"，意指「很容易達成／輕而易舉」。另一個古老諺語："from little acorns mighty oak trees grow"，「小橡實可長成巨櫟」，"Dartmoor's Piggin' Acorns" 一文的作者 Tim Sandles 認為這句諺語應當改為 "from little acorns mighty oaks trees and fat pigs grow."「小橡實可長出巨櫟，養出肥豬」。顯然 acorn（橡實）與 pigs（豬隻）自古以來就有密不可分的關係。

中世紀時的英國皇室林地或林地主人往往會在秋末准許養豬人 (swineherd) 讓豬隻到樹林裡吃落下的橡實或其他堅果，這種放養豬隻覓食橡實的傳統 (the act of pasturing swine in a wood or forest)，稱為 pannage。相對的，養豬人家在豬隻屠宰後會回饋皇家或林子主人一些豬肉，這種方式叫 in kind，英語 Pay in kind rather than in cash. (以物資代現金為報酬) 的說法，就是這麼來的。

最後這個小典故，是多年前在倫敦書展上，順手拿起一本 Penguin 出版的 The Story of Food /Food in History 部分章節抽印本看到的，偶爾看看本行以外的閒書，往往有意外的收穫。

The Luttrell Psalter - Swine herd knocking down acorns

▲ 中世紀 The Luttrell Psalter 書中養豬人將橡實敲下餵豬的插圖。

火球花
Blood Lily

單德興教授曾經在 FB 上 po 了一張中研院院區「火球花」(*Scadoxus multiflorus*, blood lily) 盛開的照片，引起大家驚豔。

「火球花」是石蒜科 (*Amaryllis family*) 網球花屬的草本植物，原產非洲，1976 以前它通行的學名是 *Haemanthus multiflorus*。*Haemanthus* 意思是「血花」(*Haema* > haima = blood 血)，(*anthus* > anthos = flower 花) (*multiflorus* = many flowers)，英文 blood lily 係源於此，有人竟然根據英文直譯為「血百合」，令人心驚。

在植物分類學上，*Haemanthus* 叫「虎耳蘭屬」，「火球花」原本歸於虎耳蘭屬，但 1838 年，自學成功、不世出的科學怪才 Rafinesque（拉芬內斯克），把它和其他幾種原來歸於虎耳蘭屬的植物獨立出來，成為的「網球花屬」(*Scadoxus*)，該屬 (genus) 有 9 個種 (species)。不過他主張的新分類，經過 138 年後的 1976 年，才為科學界確認。而根據色素體 (plastid) 的比較，「虎耳蘭屬」與「網球花屬」確實十分近似。

Rafinesque 是出生於法國的科學怪才，但後半生都在美國發展。他在動植物、地質、氣象、人類學、翻譯、語言學等方面都有傑出成就。光是 1836 年至 1838 年，他就確認了幾百個植物新屬和幾千個新種，但絕大部分未為科學界接受，因為當時世人無法賞識這位遠遠超越他所處的時代的天才學者，認為他行徑古怪，可能有精神病。

Rafinesque 把「火球花」的學名重新命名，改為 *Scadoxus multiflorus*。Scadoxus 意思是 glorious umbel（華麗的傘）(Sca > sciadon = umbrella 傘)，(doxus = glorious 華麗)。

　　最後我要提醒，「火球花」雖然美麗，但畢竟是外來植物，大家不要一窩蜂去種，因為是否會造成環境生態衝擊很難預料。還有它是石蒜科有毒植物，地下鱗莖含有多量有毒生物鹼 (poisonous alkaloids)。

▲ 火球花（單德興教授 提供）

母親的花：康乃馨與金針花
Carnation & Orange Daylily

　　美國母親節由安娜・賈維斯 (Anna Jarvis, 1864－1948) 發起，1913 年美國國會將每年 5 月的第二個星期日定為母親節，目前將近 80 個國家在這天慶祝母親節，而安娜・賈維斯的母親生前最愛的 carnation (香石竹/康乃馨) 也成了母親節的象徵。

　　康乃馨係園藝商從英文 carnation 音譯而來，它在植物學上稱為「香石竹」，學名 *Dianthus caryophyllus* 第一個字 *Dianthus*，意思是 divine flower (神聖之花)，源自希臘文 *dios* (divine) 與 *anthos* (flower)。(The scientific name of carnation is *Dianthus Caryophyllus*. *Dianthus* is derived from the Greek words for divine 'dios' and flower 'anthos'.)

　　之前介紹綬草 (*Spiranthes chinensis*) 和流蘇 (*chionanthus retusus*) 的學名時提過，學名中出現 anthes, anthos, anthus 等詞幹，都是指「花」的意思，Norton Anthology 的 anthology 也是「花的結集」的意思。

　　至於英文名稱 carnation，有學者認為是 coronation (加冕) 的訛轉。(Some scholars believe that the name 'carnation' comes from 'coronation' ... it is a corruption of coronation, from the flower's being used in chaplets (花冠) or from the toothed crown-like look of the petals.)

　　在漢字文化圈裡傳統代表母親的花是萱草 (*Hemerocallis*

fulva），古稱諼草，《詩經・衛風》：「焉得諼草，言樹之背，願言思伯，使我心痗。」唐・孟郊〈遊子詩〉：「萱草生堂階，遊子行天涯；慈母倚堂門，不見萱草花。」（諼ㄒㄩㄢ；痗ㄇㄟˋ）

萱草台灣俗稱金針花，英文名字叫 orange daylily，學名 *Hemerocallis* 是由希臘文 *hemera* (Day) 及 *kallos* (Beauty) 所組成，即「一日美人」，指它於日出開花，日落凋謝，只開一天的意思。隔日在同一花莖上會有另一朵金針花綻放。

▲ 香石竹 / 康乃馨 取自〈石竹花顏─給面小站 geimian.com〉

▲ 萱草 / 金針花 取自 kplant.biodiv.tw/ 黃花萱草

夜來花香——晚香玉及夜香木
Tuberose & Lady of the Night

　　俗稱夜來香的「晚香玉」(*Polianthes tuberosa*)，夏秋開白花，有濃香，晚上更是香味襲人 (overwhelmingly fragrant)，根部有塊莖，因此英文叫 tuberose。

　　「晚香玉」是原產墨西哥的天門冬科 (*Asparagaceae*)，龍舌蘭亞科 (*Agavoideae*) 的草本園藝植物。維基中文版說它是石蒜科，乃過時的講法。"*Polianthes* belongs to the subfamily Agavoideae of the Asparagaceae family formerly known as Agavaceae (APG III 2009). The genus is endemic to México ... among them *Polianthes tuberosa*." (AG González-Gutiérrez, 2016)"

▲ 晚香玉已開的花（張錯教授 提供）

「晚香玉」學名第一個字 *Polianthes*，意即 many flowers，學名的第二個字 *tuberosa*，即 swollen or tuberous，係指「根部腫大」之意。

晚香玉跟大蒜、韭菜一樣，開花前會抽苔，長長的花莖上帶著尚未展開的花苞，叫「晚香玉筍」，在台灣是新興蔬菜，不過在印尼晚香玉筍早就是他們的食材。吃晚香玉，聽來好像焚琴煮鶴，不過對花農這是市場調節的手法，譬如生產過剩，或當蔬菜可比花卉賣得更高價。某年夏天，北醫對面吳興街菜市場有人在賣看起來有點像蘆筍的晚香玉筍，菜販自己也不清楚那是什麼，我告訴他是晚香玉。買了一把回去清燙，頗為美味。

▲ 晚香玉筍
（取自 台北農產運銷公司網站）

晚香玉 17 世紀傳到歐洲，它那濃郁的花香，很快就成為香水原料。《凡爾賽拜金女》法王路易 16 之妻瑪麗皇后 Marie Antoinette 最愛的香水：「皇后香蹤」就散發著晚香玉的香氣。阮若缺教授 (1/29/2016) 在〈都是香水惹的禍〉文中提到「瑪麗皇后……沉溺於她最愛的香水：「皇后香蹤」(Le Sillage de la Reine)，結果成了逃亡時啟人疑竇而遭……逮捕的致命過失。」

Wikipedia mentioned that in perfumery, "Tuberose fragrances ... must be used in moderation because the essence is overpowering and can become sickly to the wearer." Mychaskiw (10/13/2017) claimed that "This Floral Note Is So Sexy, It Was Banned in the Victorian Era." 這裡的 floral note 指的是該種花的特殊芳香,因為太香了,引人想入非非,在維多利亞時代甚至遭禁。

台灣更普遍、也俗稱夜來香的植物是茄科「夜香木」*Cestrum nocturnum*,英文叫 lady of the night 或 night-blooming cestrum,原產西印度群島。夜香木學名第一個字 *Cestrum*,意即 sharpness,學名第二個字 *nocturnum*,意即 night。台灣不少社區的庭園都種有這種蔓性的灌木。流行歌《夜來香》裡所提到的芳香植物應該就是較常見的木本植物「夜香木」。

▲ 夜香木(取自 Wikipedia)

黃花風鈴木與黃鐘花
Tabebuia chrysantha & *Tecoma stans*

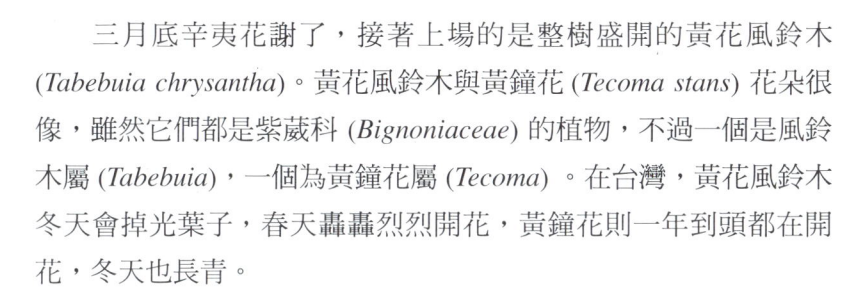

三月底辛夷花謝了,接著上場的是整樹盛開的黃花風鈴木 (*Tabebuia chrysantha*)。黃花風鈴木與黃鐘花 (*Tecoma stans*) 花朵很像,雖然它們都是紫葳科 (*Bignoniaceae*) 的植物,不過一個是風鈴木屬 (*Tabebuia*),一個為黃鐘花屬 (*Tecoma*)。在台灣,黃花風鈴木冬天會掉光葉子,春天轟轟烈烈開花,黃鐘花則一年到頭都在開花,冬天也長青。

Merriam-Webster Unabridged Dictionary 對兩者有一針見血的辨析:風鈴木是掌狀 (digitate) 複葉,黃鐘花為羽狀 (pinnate) 複葉。

Definition of *Tabebuia*

A large genus of tropical American shrubs and trees (family Bignoniaceae) having the calyx at first closed and differing from Tecoma chiefly in having digitate instead of pinnate leaves

「黃花風鈴木」(*Tabebuia chrysantha*) 學名中的種小名 *chrysantha* 即「金花」= chrys(黃金)+ antha(花)

Merriam-Webster 對風鈴木屬名 *Tabebuia* 的字源也有說明:

Origin and Etymology of *tabebuia*

New Latin, from (Tupi *tabebuya*), a tree, from (*tacyba*) ant + (*bebuya*) wood

此拉丁學名的由來大概是原產地樹上常見有螞蟻在爬的緣故

▲ 黃花風鈴木

愛文芒果與麗蠅
Irwin Mangoes & Blowflies

夏天是愛文芒果盛產的季節，台灣原有的土芒果（*Mangifera indica*）是 17 世紀荷蘭時期引進，台語稱為「檨仔」（suāinn-á），果小皮綠、肉少纖維多，但有特殊風味。

1954 年，農復會自美國佛羅里達州引進愛文（Irwin）、海頓（Haden）、肯特（Kent）、凱特（Keitt）等栽培種（cultivar），經過 7 年試種馴化，選出最適合台灣的愛文種推廣。愛文芒果皮紅肉黃，香氣濃，外表像紅蘋果一樣，所以當時又稱「蘋果檨」。

1962 年原本栽種甘蔗的台南玉井農民鄭罕池，嘗試改種愛文芒果，是台灣種植愛文芒果的先驅。愛文芒果果實碩大，皮薄肉細、香甜可口，大受消費者青睞。鄭先生很大方地將經驗傳授給其他果農，奠定玉井「愛文芒果之鄉」的美名。

但在 1960 年代末期，台南地區芒果樹大量出現開花不結果的現象，原本授粉成功的果實可達三四百公克，但若沒授粉，就無法結果，或只結如雞蛋大小的無子芒果。農政單位邀集果樹專家深入研究，經十餘年，依然未能解決。有農藝專家認為南部春季乾旱、水分不足，造成芒果不結果。台大園藝系林宗賢教授受命參與研究，進行試驗，結果加強灌水的果樹，無子芒果反而變多，推翻「水分不足造成芒果不結果」的假說。

林教授仔細觀察果園環境，發現由於果農大量栽種果樹，周遭原有次生林或草地劇減，昆蟲棲地消失，加上噴灑農藥及除草，

昆蟲幾遭趕盡殺絕。缺少昆蟲授粉，芒果樹即使開再多花也不太會結果。

1987年，有一回林教授在玉井鄉間看到居民將酬神建醮過後發臭的豬頭丟棄在芒果樹下，吸引了大群俗稱金蒼蠅的麗蠅（blowfly），注意到這些飛舞的蒼蠅附近的芒果樹都結實累累，不禁聯想，這可能是解決「開花不結果」的救星。於是林宗賢說服果農吳清進配合實驗，1988年芒果開花期間，在每八棵芒果樹中間放一堆發臭魚雜、內臟，麗蠅嗅覺非常靈敏，果園一有腐肉味，它們就會聞風而至，順帶也為芒果授粉。幾個月後芒果採收，每公頃產量達為過去的許多倍，困擾十多年的芒果開花不結果問題，終於找到解決方法。在芒果開花期間誘引麗蠅，現已成為臺灣果園量產愛文芒果的秘密武器。

今天我們有香甜可口又平價的愛文芒果可吃，應當感謝玉井農民鄭罕池的無私，台大林宗賢教授發現的秘密武器—麗蠅。

▲ 圖1 愛文芒果

▲ 圖2 麗蠅（沈競辰 攝）

In late 1960s, a large number of Irwin mango trees in Tainan area were experiencing an alarming phenomenon—they would flower but not bear fruit. A pollinated Irwin mango would weigh between 300 and 400 grams. But many mangoes weren't being pollinated, resulting in a majority of trees without mangoes.

Taiwan's Council of Agriculture formed a task force to solve the issue plaguing fruit farmers. However, more than ten years passed, and the predicament still remained unsolved.

One day in 1987, Professor Lin Tzong-Shyan saw a reeking pig head under a mango tree that had attracted hordes of blowflies, and the sounds of the large-headed flies could be heard buzzing around several mango trees nearby. Noticing an abundance of mangoes hanging from these trees, Lin Tzong-Shyan connected the dots. Could these blow flies be the savior sent to solve this issue?

During the mango flowering season of 1988, Lin Tzong-Shyan convinced a farmer to implement a grid shaped pattern in which the center area of every eight mango trees would have a pile of rotten fish or poultry viscera to attract blowflies. A few months later, the farmer had a bountiful harvest of mangoes—several times higher than that of previous years. The problem which had confounded Taiwan's Council of Agriculture for so long had finally been so creatively solved. Taiwan's mango output skyrocketed thereafter.

緬梔與梔子
Frangipani & Gardenia

緬梔（*Plumeria* spp.）是台灣常見的庭園樹木，原產中南美洲，是尼加拉瓜（Nicaragua）與寮國（Laos）的國花，花期為3-10月。

緬梔（音ㄓ）花五片花瓣外白內黃有如雞蛋，故台、港俗稱之為「雞蛋花」。中文正式名稱「緬梔」，係當年中國植物學家見它在緬甸很普遍，而「梔子」(*Gardenia jasminoides*) 是長江以南常見香花樹種，故名之。緬梔有紅花的品種，稱為「紅花緬梔」。緬梔英文一般叫 frangipani，園藝界人士則直接以屬名 Plumeria 稱之。Plumeria, the genus name is after the French botanist Charles Plumier (1646–1704).

Plumeria /pluːˈmɛriə/, known as frangipani, is a genus of flowering plants of the family Apocynaceae (夾竹桃科) endemic (特有) to Mexico, Central America, and the Caribbean, Common names for plants in the genus vary widely according to region, variety, and whim, but frangipani is the most common. Plumeria is also

▲ 圖 1 緬梔（Sandra Wu 攝）

used as a common name, especially in horticultural circles. (Adapted from Wikipedia)

16世紀時義大利貴族 Muzio Frangipane 用緬梔花製成香水，大受歡迎。加上17世紀法王路易十三（Louis XIII）喜歡這種香水，把它發揚光大，所以1675後 frangipani 作為緬梔的英文名稱在英文世界正式底定。緬梔在緬甸、寮國、泰國、柬埔寨的廟宇周遭很常見，所以有些英美人士稱之為 temple tree，但那不是正式的名稱。平常我在教學或導覽時會講要記住 frangipani 有簡單的訣竅：「本來不怕你，忽然（fran）極怕你（gipani）！」台灣常見的緬梔多是園藝雜交種，不會結果，主要以插枝繁殖。緬梔屬夾竹桃科（Apocynaceae / dogbanes）植物，修剪、折斷枝幹時流出的白色汁液有毒，沾到皮膚會發癢。

▲ 圖2 山黃梔

緬梔大約是1640年代荷蘭人引進台灣的外來植物，目的在控制瘧疾，最早大多種在池塘水岸邊，藉著花落水中來抑制蚊蟲孳生。雲林口湖鄉埔南村東南方的番樹腳，有一間小祠，供奉「荷蘭公」，廟旁有一株登錄受保護的緬梔老樹，當地傳說是荷蘭人早期在此居住時種植，距今已有370餘年。

見光華雜誌（*Taiwan Panorana*）七月號報導：

The non-native plants with the longest known history are frangipani trees (*Plumeria rubra*)...frangipani are native to Central and South America and were introduced by the Dutch into malaria-ridden Taiwan in an attempt to control mosquitoes. In the Punan community 埔南村 of Kouhu Township 口湖 in Yunlin County there is a shrine dedicated to a Dutchman, with a huge frangipani tree beside it. The statue of this "Lord Holland" wears something akin to a cowboy hat, has a handlebar moustache, yellow shirt, red pants, and ankle boots, holds a handgun, and has a happy expression on his face. Local elders say that the tree was planted by a Dutchman who came to open up this land for farming, and he was deified after passing away. Textual evidence indicates that this tree is about 370 years old.

梔子（*Gardenia jasminoides*）為常見的校園庭院植物，和咖啡樹一樣，同屬茜草科植物，葉子同樣是對生、葉脈明顯、表面翠綠光澤。梔子四季常綠，春夏開白花，然後轉黃，花極芳香，結橙黃色卵形漿果，可作為黃色染色劑。觀賞用重瓣變種大花梔子，稱為「玉堂春」，則不會結果。

Gardenia jasminoides, commonly known as gardenia, is an evergreen flowering plant in the coffee family Rubiaceae（茜草科）. It is native to parts of South-East Asia. They have very dense branches with opposite leaves（葉子對生）that are lanceolate-oblong（披針狀長橢圓形）, leathery or gathered in groups on the same node（莖節）and by a dark green, shiny and slightly waxy surface and prominent veins（葉脈明顯）.

With its shiny green leaves and heavily fragrant white summer flowers, it is widely used in gardens in warm temperate and subtropical climates. It has been in cultivation in China for at least a thousand years, and was introduced to English gardens in the mid-18th century. Many varieties have been bred for horticulture, with low-growing, and large, and long-flowering forms. (Adapted from Wikipedia)

曹銘宗先生曾在臉書上提到市售粉粿往往用人工色素染黃，

基隆活力站蒟蒻屋的粉粿則是以山梔子染色。山梔子又稱黃梔，果實是天然黃色著色劑。我小時候有種黃豆腐乾，就是塗上黃梔子的汁液加工而成，醃黃蘿蔔除用薑黃外也可以黃梔子作為黃色染劑。

　　五六十年前民間使用的染料大多是天然的，如當時漁民新編織好的棉麻漁網，都要浸染成暗赭色才能使用。通常是上山採「薯榔」（*Dioscorea rhipogonioides*）的根莖刨絲做成染料來浸泡。早期台灣灰黑色染料多取自烏桕（Chinese tallow）的葉子搗製，藍色則是取自豆科的木藍（*Indigofera tinctoria*），英文叫 true indigo，以及爵床科的馬藍（*Strobilanthes cusia*），英文名為 Assam indigo 或 Chinese rain bell。

▲ 圖 3 山黃梔花
（Susan Wang 攝）

▲ 圖 4 山黃梔果
（Susan Wang 攝）

曇花一現
Ficus racemosa & Epiphyllum oxypetalum

　　一般人會以為成語「曇花一現」的「曇花」是指夜間開花的仙人掌類植物「瓊花」。原來成語「曇花一現」出自佛經，「如是妙法，……如優曇鉢華，時一現耳。」《妙法蓮華經》，「優曇花者，此言靈瑞。三千年一現，現則金輪王出。」《法華文句》謂佛的出世、說法如優曇鉢華出現，希有難得。

　　優曇華/優曇花 (*Ficus racemosa*) 是梵語 udumbara「烏曇跋羅」之簡稱，也叫「聚果榕」，因為是隱花果，所以從外表看不到花，俗稱無花果類。三千年一現是比喻，指稀有難得。

▲ 優曇花

仙人掌類的「瓊花」(*Epiphyllum oxypetalum*, Dutchman's pipe cactus)，原產中南美洲，荷蘭人引進，在台灣本來叫「瓊花」。國府遷台後，外省人稱之為「曇花」，因為夜間開花，天亮就謝了，許多人就把它和成語「曇花一現」聯想在一起，用來表示短暫，這個成語也從原來的「稀有難得」演變成「美好事物很快就消逝」。

照片中結榕果的是優曇花，開白花的是瓊花。

▲ 瓊花

綬草
Lady's Tresses

3月底4月初，台大校園、大安森林、象山站2號出口，林安泰古厝草坪，可以見到長在平地，地生蘭類(Terrestrial Species)的「綬草」(Spiranthes chinensis) 開花，它的花序如綬帶一般，因此得名，又因為花序像一綹女孩盤繞的秀髮，所以綬草英文叫 lady's tresses。

綬草 (Spiranthes chinensis) 學名第一個字 Spiranthes 前半部 spira 意思是 coil, twist, spiral，後半的 anthes 和 anthos, anthus 一樣都指花，chinensis 即 Chinese，學名原意為 Chinese spiral flower。

綬草開花時其花序如一條紅龍盤繞在花莖上，根部似人蔘，所以又名盤龍蔘。因俗名叫「盤龍參」，公園草地上春天冒出來的綬草，常給迷信藥草食補的民眾連根挖走，進肚子。給採走的，也往往逃不過割草機的斷首。

▲ 綬草（楊銘塗教授 提供）

茄苳、重陽木、金城武樹
Javanese Bishopwood

　　幾年前媒體報導：金城武樹有「後」了！台東縣府撿子培育實生苗將送出 600 株

　　池上鄉伯朗大道上一棵堪稱台灣人氣最旺的茄苳樹—「金城武樹」，係 50 多年前鄉民吳阿木為方便拴水牛及乘涼休息在農地旁種下的。2013 藝人金城武為長榮航空拍廣告，在樹下乘涼、喝茶，一坐成名，「朝聖」人潮造就了池上旺盛的觀光業。該樹 2014 年 7 月遭麥德姆颱風 (Typhoon Matmo) 連根拔起，引發各界關注，幸經搶救，成功救回。歷經磨難後的茄苳樹生機旺盛，順利開花結果。台東縣農業處 2021 年冬天陸續派員撿拾果實，進行種子的實生苗 (seedling plant) 繁殖，培育出 600 株樹苗 (sapling)，供民眾索取。

　　Sapling 和 seedling 的區別是 sapling 係小樹苗，one not over four inches (about 10 centimeters) in diameter at breast height；seedling 是由種子長出的幼小實生苗：a young plant grown from seed; a young tree before it becomes a sapling (Merriam-Webster)。與實生苗相對的則是無性繁殖的 cutting propagation（插枝）或 graftling（嫁接苗）。

　　茄苳即重陽木 (Javanese Bishopwood, *Bischofia javanica*)，台語稱 ka-tang，清代時一般寫「加冬」，日治後變成「茄苳」。係植物學家 Karl Blume 首度在印尼爪哇採集鑑定 (1825 年)，命名為

Bischofia javanica，屬名 Bischofia 係德國植物學家 G. W. Bischoff 的姓，藉此向他致敬，種小名 (specific epithet) *javanica*，是說明採集地為爪哇。「重陽木」樹幹粗糙，樹皮赤竭，皺皺有層狀剝落及瘤狀突起，像歷盡滄桑的老人，漢字文化圈重陽節是老年節，因以名之。

不少人把「茄苳」念成 ㄑㄧㄝˊㄉㄨㄥ，但「茄苳」是從台語來的，應念為 jia dong／ㄐㄧㄚㄉㄨㄥ，普通話／國語則是「重陽木」。

「茄」字作為音譯詞時，應念 ㄐㄧㄚ，如：雪茄。就像 Nancy 的中文譯名南茜，應念作 ㄋㄢˊㄒㄧ而不是 ㄋㄢˊㄑㄧㄢˋ。

「茄苳」是台灣最普遍的原生樹種之一，有不少地方以茄苳 (ka-tang) 為名，如：佳冬鄉、茄苳村、茄苳里、茄苳路、茄苳腳、茄苳坑、茄苳林、茄苳湖、茄苳溪等，因此我們都應該知道茄苳／重陽木英文怎說—Javanese Bishopwood，簡稱 Bishopwood。

▲ 茄苳的果實

▲ 茄苳

復活節的植物：漆姑草、鳳仙、酢醬草 *The Passion in Plants: Pearlwort, Touch-me-not and the Alleluia Flower*

　　復活節每年的日期並不一致，2020 年的復活節是 4 月 12 日，當年 BBC Radio 4 播了 5 集跟耶穌受難有關的宗教民俗植物專題：*The Passion in Plants*。

　　Passion 一詞，在台灣一般只教「激情」一義，它同樣重要的另一個意思：「耶穌受難」(the suffering and death of Jesus)，大多數學生往往不知道。譬如「百香果」英文叫 passion fruit，是因為它的花 passion flower 象徵「耶穌受難」，常見有人誤以為 passion fruit 的 passion 是指「*熱情」，把它直譯為「*熱情果」。百香果 (*Passiflora edulis*) 中文正式名字叫「西番蓮」，原產熱帶美洲巴西、巴拉圭等地，17 世紀傳入歐洲，西班牙傳教士發現其花外形頗似基督釘在十字架出血形象，因此以 passioflos 名之，直譯為耶穌基督受難花 (passion flower)。

　　The Passion in Plants 的第 5 集介紹了三種跟耶穌復活有關的植物：

▲ 百香果／西番蓮花

The Resurrection - Pearlwort, Touch-me-not and the Alleluia Flower

1. 匍匐漆姑草 Pearlwort (*Sagina procumbens*)

As Christ rises from the tomb it is the pearlwort (匍匐漆姑草), according to Gaelic legend, that is there to cushion his first footfall.

耶穌走出墳墓，踏出第一步，腳踩「匍匐漆姑草」。

匍匐漆姑草，原產歐洲、西亞高海拔地區，近年來已在合歡山區武嶺附近歸化自生。匍匐漆姑草學名第二個字種小名 *procumbens* 意指植株匍匐平臥，常長成地毯狀。萼片 4，花瓣 4 或缺；台灣較常見的漆姑草 *Sagina japonica*，又稱為瓜槌草，則是萼片 5，花瓣 5。

2. 鳳仙 Touch-me-not (*Impatiens balsamina*)

One of the most beautiful stories of the Resurrection is that of Mary Magdalene meeting the risen Christ and mistaking him for the gardener. As she reaches out towards him, he tells her not to touch

▲ 漆姑草 (萼片 5，花瓣 5)（陳文彬 提供）

▲ 漆姑草 vs 匍匐漆姑草（萼片 4，花瓣 4 或缺，引自 福星花園）

him. This Biblical story is told again in the name of the 'touch-me-not' balsam.

鳳仙花叫 touch-me-not 的美麗故事：抹大拉的瑪麗亞誤以為復活的耶穌是園丁，要靠近時，耶穌告訴她「別碰我」，這則聖經故事就這樣和鳳仙花聯繫在一起。

3. 山酢醬草 Wood sorrel (*Oxalis acetosella*)

In the culmination of the story, they find in the woods at Hilfield friary, the beautiful wood sorrel. Flowering at Easter, it is known as the 'Alleluia plant'.

在英國及歐洲許多地方，復活節也是「山酢醬草」開花的時節，因此山酢醬草又稱為 Alleluia Plant。

「山酢醬草」英文名稱 wood sorrel 的 wood 指樹林，sorrel 指「酸模」(*Rumex acetosa*)，因為酢醬草味道酸酸像「酸模」。

▲ 鳳仙花（引自 kplant.biodiv.tw）

開小黃花的酢醬草 (Yellow Woodsorrel, *Oxalis stricta*) 是臺灣及歐亞大陸的原生植物，臺灣更常見花朵醒目的「紫花酢醬草」(Pink Woodsorrel, *Oxalis corymbosa*)，則是原產南美洲的歸化植物。

▲ 山酢醬草

根據《重編國語辭典修訂本》第六版「酢漿草」的讀音 ㄘㄨˋ ㄐㄧㄤ ㄘㄠˇ cù jiāng cǎo

▲ 酢醬草（蘇恆隆 攝）

▲ 紫花酢醬草（蘇恆隆 攝）

福木
Fukugi Tree

　　菲島福木 (*Garcinia subelliptica*) 俗稱「福木」，中文名稱源自日文 Fukugi，福 (ふく) + 木 (き)，英文稱為 Happiness Tree 或 Fukugi Tree，菲島福木的屬名 Garcinia 是紀念自然學家 Laurent Garcin 對採集亞洲熱帶植物的貢獻。The genus is named after Franco-Swiss naturalist Laurent Garcin (1683–1751)，種名 *subelliptica* 是指葉子近乎橢圓 (means more or less elliptic, referring to the shape of the leaf)。

　　菲島福木與極受歡迎的東南亞水果——山竹 (*Garcinia mangostana,* Mongosteen) 都是藤黃科 *Garcinia* 屬植物。菲島福木原產於菲律賓、台灣、琉球群島等地，臺灣主要分布於蘭嶼與綠島海濱地區。

Commonly known as the Fukugi Tree, *Garcinia subelliptica* is related to the common mangosteen. It is an evergreen tree found in coastal forests of East and Southeast Asia, specifically the Ryukyu Islands of Japan, Taiwan, Philippines, Indonesia, Sri Lanka, and India.

▲ Some of the Fukugi fruit I collected in August 2023

Trees are 6–20 meters high with ovate-oblong or elliptical thick leathery leaves. Its fruit turns yellow when ripe and emits a strong and pungent scent.

福木葉子光滑，十字對生，長橢圓形，是典型的革質葉。乳黃色花多叢生於葉腋。果為球形漿果，熟時橙黃色，會散發瓦斯的臭味，果實內有 2-4 枚褐色種子。因枝葉茂密，不易落葉，樹形優美，呈圓錐形，適合作為景觀園藝、防音、防風 (windbreak) 樹種，學校、公園或行道皆可見其蹤影。四、五月為盛花期，八九月結果實，球形漿果口感如甜柿，成熟時會產生類似榴槤般氣味。若能加以改良，可望成為優良商業量產果樹。

▲ Fukugi fruit falling all over the ground in August 2024

楓香
Formosan Sweet Gum

楓香 (Formosan Sweet Gum) 是楓香科 (Altingiaceae) 楓香屬 (Liquidambar) 的落葉喬樹木，樹形優美，葉掌狀三裂 (have three lobes)，互生 (alternate)，葉初生時紫紅，之後轉深綠，秋冬時葉子變黃，在高海拔及較冷地區則葉子變紅。

When young, sweet gum leaves are purplish-red, but turn dark green during the growing season. In the fall, they turn yellow-red in the south and red in the north.

▲ 圖 1 左上方為楓香雌花序，小花柱頭 2 分叉、紅色；其餘皆為雄花序（陳文彬 提供）

203

▲ 圖 2 楓香刺球型的聚合果，spherical, spiny fruiting heads, known as gumballs （陳文彬 提供）

　　楓香產於平地至海拔 2,000 公尺地區，台灣中部埔里至霧社間山區往往成純林。楓香樹皮受傷後流出的樹脂稱「楓香脂」(Sweet Gum Resin)，可入藥。葉可飼天蠶蛾 (*Saturnia* spp.) 幼蟲。木材可做建材、香菇之段木，果實即中藥之「路路通」。

　　楓香是雌雄同株 (monoecious)，春初萌發新葉時，先長出黃綠色的短穗狀雄花序，不久即掉落，之後才出現圓球形的雌花序，以避免花粉落到同一株的雌花上，增加遺傳多樣性。

　　Yellow-green male flowers appear before female flowers and fall off. Female flowers eventually develop into spherical spiny fruiting clusters.

Liquidambar 由 liquidus（汁液）與 ambar（琥珀）組成，意指其樹皮受傷後會流出琥珀色的汁液。這種汁液若埋到地底久了形成化石，就是琥珀。

"*Liquidus*" means liquid and "*ambar*" means amber, so *Liquidambar* is virtually liquid amber (fossil tree resin). Both the scientific and common names refer to the sweet resinous sap (liquid amber) exuded by the trunk when cut.

楓香主要生長在氣候溫暖地帶，日本出土的中新世楓香化石證明，兩千多萬年前日本青森、長崎等地區也有楓香，後來氣候大變遷後，楓香消失了。日本治台期間，發現台灣有許多原生楓香，基於補償心理，就開始大種楓香，溫州街台大宿舍區以前兩旁都種了楓香，大概是這樣的原因。

楓香葉子互生，揉碎有芒果的香味，而楓樹 (Maple, *Acer* spp.) 的葉片則兩兩對生，葉子沒有特殊香氣。楓香屬 *Liquidambar* 從前歸類於金縷梅科 (*Hamamelidaceae*)，現在併入新成立的楓香科 (*Altingiaceae*)。楓屬 (*Acer*) 又名槭屬，通稱為楓樹、槭樹，以前歸於槭樹科 (*Aceraceae*)，但是根據最近分子生物學研究 (phylogenetic studies)，將它歸到無患子科中。

杜牧《山行》「遠上寒山石徑斜，白雲生處有人家；停車坐愛楓林晚，霜葉紅於二月花。」詩中的「楓林」，指的應該是楓樹 (Maple, *Acer* spp.)，而不是楓香樹 (*Liquidambar*, Sweet Gum)。

木棉與吉貝木棉
Kapok & Cotton Tree

每年三月起又是木棉花的季節，全台各地的木棉枝頭上都高高舉著著橘紅的火炬，極為壯麗。

木棉原產印度、馬來群島，樹幹基部密生瘤刺，以防動物攀爬啃食。掌狀複葉，叢聚枝梢，小葉 5～7 片。側枝輪生於主幹四週。花碩大橘紅，花期在 3 月至 4 月初。木棉花是高雄的市花，金門的縣樹。在中國大陸則是廣州市及潮州市等四個城市的市花。

▲ 木棉 (J.M.Garg, Wikimedia)

台灣的英文媒體在報導木棉 (*Bombax ceiba*) 時往往誤稱為 *kapok，其實 kapok 中文叫「吉貝木棉」(*Ceiba pentandra*)，年初開花，花朵黃白色，比木棉花小很多。中文「吉貝」就是學名 Ceiba，英文 kapok 的音譯。木棉英文是 cotton tree，red silk-cotton，或 red cotton tree。

▲ 吉貝木棉花黃白，簇生枝梢（Wikipedia）

木棉 (*Bombax ceiba*) "is commonly known as cotton tree. More specifically, it is sometimes known as red silk-cotton or red cotton tree" (Wikipedia)

2014 年英語教育專家 Wiley Blevins，在臺大活動中心演講完後，我帶他逛臺大校園，解說花草樹木的各種生存策略，如木棉樹的瘤刺，榕屬植物的氣根與纏勒，白千層的樹皮，他聽得入迷，跟我說，「Jerome, 我決定要寫一本青少年讀物，介紹植物的神奇。」沒想到三年後，書真的問世了。他寄來一本樣書 *Ninja Plants: Survival and Adaptation in the Plant World*。書的扉頁上赫然印著一行獻詞：To Jerome Su, who inspired this book after our walk through the campus grounds of National Taiwan University. 讓我覺得與有榮焉。

▲ 木棉花去蒂及花蕊，留下花瓣

木棉花可以食用，是緬甸、泰國、印度傳統飲食中的食材。

In Myanmar (緬甸), its flowers are dried and cooked. They are one of the traditional foods of Myanmar. In India, the flower-bud is eaten as a vegetable.

▲ 木棉花魚丸湯

The dry cores of the Bombax ceiba (木棉) flower are an essential ingredient of the nam ngiao spicy noodle soup (辣湯麵，成分有木棉花乾，蕃茄，碎猪肉，香料，辣椒等) in Shan State (撣邦) and Northern Thailand, as well as the kaeng khae curry (假蒟咖哩). Its flower buds are also used in regional cuisine of Southern India as a spice as well as herbal medicine. (Wikipedia)

木棉花去蒂及中間的花蕊，留下五片花瓣，可以三吃：1. 開水氽燙，淋美乃滋；2. 加桂圓煮甜湯；3. 加排骨、貢丸或魚丸煮湯。

▲ 木棉花沙拉

▲ 木棉花桂圓湯

肉豆蔻、小豆蔻、豆蔻年華
Nutmeg/Mace & Cardamom

最近朋友請喝印度奶茶，飲料有特殊香味，我女兒說裏頭加了 cardamom，我同事說那是豆蔻，我愣了一下，因為我印象中豆蔻不是 nutmeg 嗎？後來花了一番工夫查證，原來「豆蔻」至少可指涉七種以上植物：

印度傳統奶茶、印度咖哩、中東料理常用的豆蔻香料是小豆蔻 (True cardamom, *Elettaria cardamomum*)，是小豆蔻屬植物 (Elettaria)，也叫綠豆蔻 (green cardamom)，見下圖。

Cardamom (/ˈkɑːrdəməm/) is a spice made from the seeds of several plants in the genera *Elettaria* (小豆蔻屬植物) and *Amomum* (豆蔻屬植物) in the family Zingiberaceae (薑科). Both genera are

▲ 小豆蔻 / 綠豆蔻 (*Elettaria cardamomum*)

native to the Indian subcontinent and Indonesia. They are recognized by their small seed pods: triangular in cross-section and spindle-shaped, with a thin, papery outer shell and small, black seeds; *Elettaria* pods are light green and smaller, while *Amomum* pods are larger and dark brown. (Wikipedia)

香豆蔻 (*Amomum subulatum*),也叫黑豆蔻 black cardamom,是豆蔻屬植物,通常不用於甜食上,見下圖。

Amomum subulatum, also known as Black cardamom, has a different flavor. Unlike green cardamom, it is rarely used in sweet dishes. Its smoky flavor and aroma derive from traditional methods of drying over open flames. (Wikipedia)

成語「豆蔻年華」源於唐代詩人杜牧的詩:「娉娉嫋嫋十三餘,豆蔻梢頭二月初。春風十里揚州路,卷上珠簾總不如。」杜牧用二月枝頭含苞待放的豆蔻花來形容十三四歲清純的美麗少女,

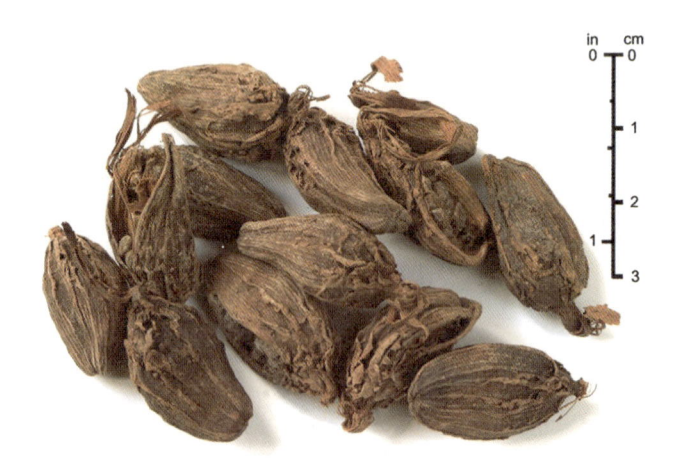

▲ 香豆蔻 / 黑豆蔻 (*Amomum subulatum*) Black Cardamom seed pods. (Photograph by Brian Arthur)

▲ 月桃 (*Alpinia zerumbet*) shell ginger（引自 陳文彬《新細說台灣原生植物》）

豆蔻花具體是指哪一種植物，已很難查考了，不過根據文獻描述，大概是薑科月桃屬（中國大陸稱為山薑屬）植物 (shell ginger)，見上圖。

肉荳蔻 (*Myristica fragrans*) 為肉豆蔻科肉豆蔻屬的香料樹，果實成熟會裂開，黑褐色種子去殼，裡面的種仁叫 nutmeg；肉豆蔻種子外包覆的紅色假種皮 (aril)，乾燥後像魷魚乾，顏色淡橘黃，叫 mace。種仁及假種皮都可做為香料（見圖 1 & 2）。Two spices derived from its fruit: nutmeg, from its seed, and mace, from the seed covering (aril).

總之，中文豆蔻可指以下七種植物，除肉豆蔻外，其餘六種都是薑科植物：

▲ 圖 1 肉豆蔻果實成熟會裂開：紅色部分為假種皮（aril），黑色種子裡的種仁為肉豆蔻 (nutmeg)；圖 2 為乾燥後的假種皮，稱為 mace。（圖取自 Wikipedia）

肉豆蔻 (*Myristica fragrans*) 肉豆蔻屬 *Myristica*；

小豆蔻 / 綠豆蔻 (*Elettaria cardamomum*) 小豆蔻屬 *Elettaria*；

紅豆蔻 (*Alpinia galanga*) Greater Galangal (大高良薑)；

豆蔻 / 草豆蔻 (*Alpinia hainanensis/ Alpinia katsumadai*) 海南山薑，月桃屬 *Alpinia*；

香豆蔻 / 黑豆蔻 (*Amomum subulatum*) 豆蔻屬 *Amomum*；

白豆蔻 (*Wurfbainia vera*) Siam cardamom 砂仁屬 *Wurfbainia*；

爪哇白豆蔻 (*Wurfbainia compacta*) 砂仁屬 *Wurfbainia*

中文同一名稱指涉幾種不同植物的例子還不少，杏仁可以指 apricot kernel，也可以指 almond，杏仁豆腐、杏仁露其實是 apricot kernel 製成的，與 almond 無關。茴香也是一個例子，可能指繖形科的 fennel，也可能指 star anise (八角茴香)。

杏仁豆腐、杏仁茶英文怎麼說？ Apricot Kernel & Almond

多年前我去臺南市政府協助審訂「臺南市民英語資源網」英語菜單翻譯，其中「杏仁茶」原譯 almond tea，擬改為 almond milk，我建議改為 apricot kernel drink；「杏仁豆腐」原譯 almond tofu，擬改為 almond jelly，我主張改為 apricot kernel jelly，審議會接受了我的建議。

「杏仁」是典型很容易引起混淆的「一名多物」現象 (polysemy)。杏仁豆腐、杏仁茶的主要原料，以及中藥裡常用的「杏仁」(the common use of apricot kernels as a component in traditional Chinese medicine)，是「杏」(apricot) 的種仁 (kernel) 製成的，usually, from the species *Prunus armeniaca*；而堅果的「杏仁」則是 the edible and widely cultivated seed of almond (Prunus dulcis)。

中藥杏仁有時又有南杏、北杏之分，但南、北杏基本上都是同一種水果 apricot 的變種，杏仁是它們的種仁 (kernel)，與堅果的 almond 不同。北杏較苦，含氰化物 (cyanide) 量較高。

▲ Apricot Kernels

Almond 類與 apricot 係同一屬，但不同種。Almond 的果實沒什麼果肉，所以主要是吃它多脂的種子。有人主張 almond 應改名為「巴丹杏」，因為在印度叫 badam，在中國大陸就稱為「巴丹杏」。

　　植物的俗名除了有一名多物 (polysemy) 的現象，更常見的是「一物多名」(synonymy)，譬如錦葵科木槿屬的 *Hibiscus rosa-sinensis*，一般叫「朱槿」，又有赤槿、佛桑、扶桑、桑槿、火紅花、照殿紅、大紅花、燈籃仔花……等十幾種名稱。

　　在學術上為方便交流和避免一物多名或一名多物的問題，物種的學名全世界都通用拉丁雙名法 (binomial nomenclature) 的名稱。按照這 two-term naming system，每個學名都由屬名 (genus) 和種加詞 (specific epithet) 兩部分構成。如「杏仁果」almond 學名第一字 *Prunus* 係屬名，第一個字母要大寫，第二個字 *dulcis* 則是種加詞，小寫，意思是 sweet, pleasant，屬名、種加詞，兩個字都要斜體。

▲ Almonds

芋頭與南島民族
Taro & Austronesian Peoples

　　我曾在《南島誌 Ora Nui》新書發表會上，簡短的講述「芋頭」的英文 taro 與南島語言的關係，以及南島民族對「甘蔗」sugarcane 傳播全球的貢獻。

　　近 20 年的南島遷移理論支持南島民族 (Austronesian peoples) 係四千多年前由台灣遷移到太平洋其他地區。南島語系也是全世界最大的語系之一。Wikipedia 的 Domesticated Plants and Animals of Austronesia 一則中提到，四千多年前開始的南島民族遷徙，從台灣飄洋過海帶到各地的植物包括甘蔗與芋頭。底下是「芋頭」的部分，「甘蔗」容後再述。

▲ 芋頭（taro）與小芋頭（eddo）
（圖出自 clovegarden.com）

The English term taro (芋頭) was borrowed from the Maori language of New Zealand (紐西蘭毛利語) when Captain Cook (庫克船長) first observed plantations of *Colocasia* (芋頭) tubers there in 1769. The form taro or talo is widespread among Polynesian languages (玻里尼西亞語): taro in Tahitian; talo in Samoan; kalo in Hawaiian; ta o in Marquesan. All these forms originate from Proto-Polynesian *talo, which itself descended from Proto-Oceanic *talos (cf. dalo in Fijian) and Proto-Austronesian (古南島語/原始南島語) *tales (cf. tales in Javanese). It's 芋 (ō) or 芋頭 (ō-á) in Taiwanese, vasa in Paiwan, and tali in Amis (阿美語).

Taro were carried into the Pacific Islands (太平洋群島) by Austronesian peoples (南島民族) from around 1300 BC, where they became a staple crop (主要作物) of Polynesians. Taro is also one of the staples of Micronesia (密克羅尼西亞). Taro pollen (芋頭花粉) and starch residue (芋頭澱粉殘跡) have also been identified in Lapita sites, dated to between 1100 BC and 550 BC. Taro was later spread to Madagascar (馬達加斯加) as early as the 1st century AD. 以上英文部分節錄自 Wikipedia。

英文裡「小芋頭」又叫 eddo 或 eddoe，以前植物學家認為「小芋頭」(*Colocasia antiquorum*) 與「芋頭」(*Colocasia esculenta*) 同屬但不同種，後來多認為 eddo 與 taro 是同屬又同種，都是 *Colocasia esculenta*。

英文 eddo 一詞可能源自漢語「芋頭」，根據 Wikipedia：

Eddoes appear to have been developed as a crop in China and Japan and introduced from there to the West Indies where they are sometimes called "Chinese eddoes."

柿子挑軟的吃
Go For Easy Pickings

　　十月是柿子盛產的季節,幾十年前傳統的脆柿,如石柿、牛心柿,果實內含有大量的單寧(tannin),需要以石灰水浸泡脫澀,又要去皮,才能食用;相較之下,軟柿(以電石催熟後的四周柿/正柿),皮薄肉軟,可直接食用,因此有「柿子挑軟的吃」的說法。

　　「柿子挑軟的吃」這句話又引申人就是喜歡挑簡單容易的事來做,想佔人便宜的時候,也總是找那些好欺負的。

　　「柿子挑軟的吃」做為比喻,相當於英文的 go for easy pickings。見以下數例:

▲ 左為富有種甜柿,右邊為軟柿。

- But I think most people go for easy pickings, maybe just to save time, or because there's⋯, whatever.

- Predators go for easy pickings

- Bike thieves always go for easy pickings first.

- But they don't want to be caught in the act, so burglars generally go for easy pickings. A property that looks empty or one with lax security are the ones most vulnerable to break-ins.

My English teacher 網站說明這個成語的由來：(Anastasia Koltai, Nov 14, 2019)

This phrase dates back to the late 16th century when thieves and "pickpocketers" would identify and target people and places they thought would be easy to steal from.

現在市面上賣的柿子大多為日本引進又甜又脆的富有種甜柿，傳統的脆柿，因為要脫澀處理才能販售，已少有人種植。

甜品葷與素：吉利丁、果膠與瓊膠 Gelatin, Pectin & Agar

有人問：甜品也有葷素之別嗎？利用這機會來談一下吉利丁、果膠與瓊膠的差別，以及其相對應的英文。

明膠 / 吉利丁 (gelatin)

吉利丁(明膠)係由牛、豬皮骨或結締組織提煉的，是一種淺黃色透明、無味的膠原蛋白，一般以片狀或粉狀販售，常用於製作果凍、布丁等甜品。(Gelatin is a translucent, colorless, flavorless food ingredient, commonly derived from collagen taken from the skins, connective tissues, and bones of cattle and pigs. It's often a key ingredient of desserts and candies.) 除食品加工、家庭烹飪外，也是藥物、化妝品的凝膠劑 (gelling agent)。如果吃素，用明膠 / 吉利丁製作的果凍及布丁等甜品就不宜了。

果膠 (pectin)

果膠 (pectin) 是由植物提煉的，是一種水溶性纖維，能夠形成凝膠 (gel)，果膠能結合腸道中的物質，增加糞量，亦可減少身體從食物中吸收的膽固醇量。用於烹飪、烘焙，可作為增稠劑 (thickener)，亦可用於製藥。

Pectin is a soluble fiber (polysaccharide) found in fruits. It is used as a thickener in cooking and baking. It is also sometimes used to make medicine. Pectin binds substances in the

▲ 愛玉 (*Ficus pumila* var. *awkeotsang*) （陳文彬 提供）

intestines and adds bulk to the stools. It might also reduce how much cholesterol the body absorbs from foods.

(PECTIN - Uses, Side Effects, and More – WebMD)

果膠存在於蔬果等天然食物中，譬如薜（ㄅㄧˋ）荔 (*Ficus pumila*) 及其變種愛玉 (*Ficus pumila* var. *awkeotsang*) 就富含果膠。The mature fruits of climbing figs such as *Ficus pumila* and *Ficus pumila* var. *awkeotsang* are rich in pectin.

瓊膠 / 洋菜 (agar)

瓊膠 / 瓊脂，又稱洋菜，是石花菜 (*Gelidium amansii*) 之類的海藻加熱溶化，冷卻凝固而成的。在實驗室進行微生物研究，培養皿通常會充填 agar-agar 作為培養基。

▲ 內含 agar-agar 的細菌培養皿 (Wikipedia)

Agar (/ˈeɪɡɑːr/ or /ˈɑːɡər/), or agar-agar, is a jelly-like substance consisting of polysaccharides obtained from the cell walls of some species of red algae, primarily from "ogonori" (*Gracilaria*) and "tengusa" (Gelidiaceae). (Wikipedia)

因此如果吃素，製作果凍及布丁等甜品就只能用果膠與瓊膠了，而相對於果膠與明膠，瓊膠/洋菜的凝膠結構更強。Agar has a stronger gel structure compared to gelatin and pectin.

野菜
Foraging Wild Edible Plants

許多路旁、庭院、校園裡我們必欲除之而後快、稱為雜草的植物，其實是可食用的救荒植物，有些還挺美味呢！

Many edible wild plants are the ones we pull out of our yards or campuses all the time and we call them "weeds."

雨後野菜往往長得特別茂盛，但常放晴沒幾天就給拔除了。以下幾種是我常採來加菜的野蔬：

These are just a few examples of the wild plants I like to forage in my neighborhood.

綠莧 (*Amaranthus viridis*, green amaranth)，又稱野莧，學名第一個字 *Amaranthus*，本意是 unfading flower，是莧的屬名 (genus name)；第二個字，*viridis*，是種小名 (specific epithet)，意思是綠色。綠莧在台灣荒地、路旁，隨處可見，其嫩莖、嫩葉、花穗、種子皆可食用，可炒、煮或汆燙，較一般市售的莧菜可口，也更耐放。野莧春夏季生長旺盛，可作為救荒作物。

▲ 綠莧 （圖片來源自 Wikipedia）

Amaranthus viridis is a cosmopolitan species in the family *Amaranthaceae*, commonly known as green amaranth. It is an annual herb with an upright, light green stem that grows to about 60–80 cm in height. *Amaranthus viridis* is eaten as a boiled green or as a vegetable in many parts of the world. Green amaranth has clusters of nutty edible seeds that can be easily harvested by scraping the ripe spikes of seeds between the fingers.

龍葵 (*Solanum nigrum*, black nightshade)，又稱烏甜仔菜、烏籽仔菜，是路旁、庭園、野地常見的茄科茄屬草本植物，葉子互生，卵形或長橢圓型；夏初開白色小花，球形漿果，成熟後黑紫色，可食。但未成熟果為綠色，含龍葵鹼 (solanine) 不可食用。龍葵葉子及嫩莖可煮、可炒，略帶點苦味，如不喜歡苦味可先用開水汆燙再煮。學名中 *Solanum* 是指茄屬，*nigrum* 意指黑色。

▲ 龍葵 （圖片來源自 Wikipedia）

Solanum nigrum, black nightshade or blackberry nightshade, is a species of flowering plant in the family Solanaceae, native to Eurasia. Ripe black nightshade berries have a sweet and savory flavor and can be eaten raw. The young leaves and stems can be boiled or stir fried and have an herbal, grassy flavor.

▲ 長梗滿天星　（本書作者 攝）

　　長梗滿天星 / 空心蓮子草 (*Alternanthera philoxeroides*, alligator weed)，為莧科草本植物，生長在野地、園圃、溝渠旁，通常一長就是一整片。低窪濕地族群尤其繁茂，開花時有如繁星點點。莖管狀空心，基部匍匐，上部斜向生長 (stems sprawling along ground, curving upward)。葉對生，倒卵形 (opposite leaves oval-shaped and thinner at base)，近乎無柄。頭狀花序圓球形，白色。已開花部位的莖通常比較老，宜採未開花部位的嫩莖葉，可煮、可炒，類似空心菜。

　　Alternanthera philoxeroides, is an invasive species in the family Amaranthaceae, commonly referred to as alligator weed. It can thrive in both dry and aquatic environments and is characterized by whitish, papery flowers along its short stalks. Alligator weed has sprawling hollow stems with opposite leaves sprouting from its nodes. Its tender stems and fleshy leaves can be cooked.

檳榔、半天花、半天筍、荖藤的英文 Betel Nut Flowers & Betel Nut Shoots

betel 是什麼？

之前有位老師來信，說我主編的《麥克米倫英漢雙解辭典》以下英文定義有誤："betel: a plant of Southeast Asia with leaves that people chewed"，他說檳榔葉怎麼嚼？他以為「檳榔」是 betel nut，那 betel 就當然是「檳榔樹」了。不！betel 是「荖藤」，不是「檳榔」或「檳榔樹」。

「檳榔」(betel nut) 是「檳榔樹」(betel palm) 的果實，而「荖藤」，又名「蔞葉」則是胡椒科藤本植物 *Piper betle*，用來包在檳榔外面，咀嚼時增加興奮刺激效果，這種包荖藤葉的檳榔較貴，稱「包葉檳榔」。

▲ 檳榔　　　　　　　　　　　▲ 包葉檳榔

Collins English Dictionary 對 betel（荖藤）有詳細的解釋：an Asian piperaceous climbing plant, *Piper betle*, the leaves of which are chewed, with the betel nut, by the peoples of SE Asia.

▲ 荖藤

半天花 (betel nut flowers)、半天筍 (betel nut shoots)

「半天花」與「半天筍」是近年新興的食材。「半天花」就是檳榔的花序；檳榔樹幹頂端嫩芽、嫩葉及嫩莖為葉鞘所包覆的部份，剝去葉鞘外皮後組織尚未老化的檳榔心，則稱為「半天筍」。

傳統市場 4-6 月有時可見販售「半天花」與「半天筍」，可煮可炒，做成佳餚，口感爽脆，猶如嫩筍。不過因含有 Arecoline 等檳榔鹼，不宜一次超過 250 公克。熟悉台灣文化的 Ian Bartholomew 也曾在 Taipei Times 介紹過半天花，可做為介紹台灣特色美食的英文教材。

▲ 炒半天花美食
（感謝張錯教授分享）

Intoxicating flowers -
https://www.taipeitimes.com › archives › 2018/06/23
Jun 23, 2018 — Betel nut flowers are a Taiwan delicacy, but be aware that they might provide you with more than just a good source of dietary fiber.

後語

　　自 1996 年以來，我帶領植物愛好者走訪自然，至今已有數百場，許多參加者希望我能把解說內容形諸筆墨出版，但我不諳打字，又恐災梨禍棗，沒有出書的念頭。2016 年我的助理林玉茵幫我建立臉書帳號及打字，她離職後，沈愛萍接續這項工作，陸續把我對翻譯及植物的一些心得，化為一篇篇筆記，星散於臉書上，如今集結成書，終於不負多年來殷殷敦促的朋友期待。

　　整理這些寫過的文章比較耗時的是，考證植物的最新學名與英文名稱，筆者反覆查證，力求資訊正確，希望對從事翻譯、中英雙語教學、自然解說者有所幫助。譬如稜果榕 (*Ficus septica*) 至少有四種英文俗名，Wikipedia 收錄的是 Hauili fig，係由於修正前的學名是 *Ficus hauilii*，我參考 Plants of the World / Kew Science，只收按學名直譯的 Septic Fig，以及 White-veined Fig，讀者可從英文名稱了解稜果榕的特徵是有明顯的白色葉脈 (white-veined)。

　　本書得以完成，仰賴眾多人的支持與幫助：特別感謝《看見台灣原生植物》、《細說台灣原生植物》的作者陳文彬先生同意轉載許多植物的照片；以及鄭杏倩女士提供精心繪製的植物插畫，封面上結著蘋果的台灣欒樹，即是鄭老師所繪製。

　　此外，感謝蘇恆隆、楊銘塗教授、張錯教授惠借照片，李有成教授、王安琪教授、陳東榮教授給予寶貴的回饋，以及書林同仁張雅雯積極催稿。

　　本書記錄了過去幾年的走讀旅程，彙整我分享過的植物故事，衷心期盼能讓更多讀者留意這方土地上的一花一木，關注人文與自然的連結。